GRACED VULNERABILITY

 A Theology of Childhood

DAVID   H.   JENSEN

The Pilgrim Press Cleveland

for Hannah Grace

The Pilgrim Press, 700 Prospect Avenue, Cleveland, Ohio 44115-1100
thepilgrimpress.com
© 2005 David H. Jensen

Scripture quotations, unless otherwise noted, are from the New Revised
Standard Version of the Bible, © 1989 by the Division of Christian Education
of the National Council of Churches of Christ in the United States of America
and are used by permission. Changes have been made for inclusivity.

Printed in the United States of America on acid-free paper

10   09   08   07   06   05   5   4   3   2   1

Library of Congress Cataloging-in-Publication Data

Jensen, David Hadley, 1968–
    Graced vulnerability : a theology of childhood / David H. Jensen.
        p.   cm.
    Includes bibliographical references.
    ISBN 0-8298-1621-6 (pbk. : alk. paper)
    1. Children (Christian theology)   I. Title.
BT705.J46   2005
233—dc22

2005043027

CONTENTS

Foreword

n overabundance of libelous bumper stickers cluttered the 2004 presidential campaign on all political fronts. One of the more troubling read "Don't be a *girly-man;* vote Republican," coming from the Republican convention. Along with fear of women and gays, an even deeper fear—that of human vulnerability—motivated this slogan. The highest reward, it seemed, would go to the candidate who could appear the most "manly-man."

Such a context makes David Jensen's powerful reclamation of "graced vulnerability" among children and adults all the more important. "Consider the Children" is the title of first chapter. This itself is a radical shift. The general public has come to expect little from academic theology on matters so close to home, especially children. When systematic theologians of the last century spoke about human nature and redemption, they meant, without hesitation, *adult* nature and *adult* redemption. The social sciences and self-help books easily cornered the market. Whether one wants to know how to weather pregnancy, increase a child's intelligence, or deal with a depressed teen, one turns unquestionably to such sources. Children have simply not been proper subject matter for theology, not because they were unimportant but, more simply, because they had vanished from the sight of the typical male theologian, sequestered in his study and not directly responsible for the daily grind of child care.

Until recently. The past few years have seen a remarkable rebirth of interest in children among religion scholars. Jensen's rich exposition of children's vulnerability is a wonderful addition to this growing discussion. From its reclamation of the vulnerable Ishmael to its reconsideration of the vulnerability of sin to its promotion of particular ecclesial practices of vulnerability, this book contains insights that prove the so-called pedestrian topic of children to be anything but mundane.

Jensen's primary claim is that children's vulnerability exemplifies our basic humanity and God's own nature: "By becoming vulnerable with the children in our midst, we not only stake a claim with their lives, we also understand more fully what it means to be created in God's image and what it means to be church." To be vulnerable means "to expose oneself to possible harm and injury." But it also means to acknowledge dependence on and connection with others. Adults repress vulnerability and some even declare, through bumper stickers or otherwise, their outright distaste. But they do not ultimately "outgrow it." Indeed, vulnerability is not just constitutive of children's nature; it is a primary characteristic of God in relationship to us.

Many people are not going to like this "good news" any more than they like the threat of becoming a "girly-man." But as Jensen urges, "theology matters." It matters whether people picture God as a war-waging monarch who secures military victory over his (male pronoun intended) opponents or as a vulnerable child.

Do not, Jensen cautions, idealize or romanticize this vulnerability. Raw vulnerability, unprotected and ignored, quickly degenerates. Many statistics Jensen cites are incomprehensible. One in three children worldwide live below subsistence level, with the annual income of developed countries one hundred times greater than undeveloped. Forty percent of children under age six in the United States live in low-income families. Children in the United States make up 71 percent of all sex crime victims. The United States is only one of six nations to condone capital punishment of juvenile offenders and has executed the highest number. In the decade from 1990 to 2000, two million children were killed by warfare, with the United States the largest supplier of destructive arms. Such vulnerability is not to be condoned; it must be confronted and radically rectified.

Graced Vulnerability offers three essential avenues of redress: scriptural, doctrinal, and practical. As vividly seen in both the cry of Ishmael, whom Hagar has placed in the shelter of the bushes, unable to bear the sight of his death from thirst, hunger, and heat, and in Jesus' invitation to children in the gospels, a child's vulnerability is the "locus of God's grace." The "God who becomes vulnerable in relationship with Israel," argues Jensen, "calls the covenant people to become vulnerable to those on the margins." God suffers, mourns, reproaches, and demands renewed commitment to this covenant. Care for the vulnerable—the "widow, orphan, and stranger"—stands at its center. We are commanded to love the "alien" because we all were once "aliens in the land of Egypt" (Lev. 19:33–34).

This demand is echoed in the New Testament. God enters human history not in the blazing triumph, safety, and global security of a mission accomplished but in meager surroundings and "public disgrace" (Matt. 1:18) at the margins of society, precarious and already marked for murder. In turn, Jesus' ministry touches the most vulnerable—"those whom others will not touch."

The cross ultimately exemplifies the world's intolerance for such a God. So Jensen turns from scripture to the doctrine of atonement. On the cross hangs a God torn by anguish, the "tragedy of a Savior who becomes vulnerable for the world." God suffers that which renders us powerless and triumphs. To "consider children" also suggests that the classic understanding of sin "falls short" of the "haunting circumstances" of many children. All too often religious tradition defines sin from the perspective of those in power and seldom from the "underside." Any adequate definition must include both actor and the acted upon—the position most often occupied by children.

Ultimately, however, "graced vulnerability" relies upon familial and ecclesial practice. The church has longstanding traditions that affirm a different kind of power, security, and trust than the world typically recognizes. Jensen explores four such "practices of vulnerability"—baptism, peacemaking, sanctuary, and prayer. Baptism sanctions our embodied vulnerability before God, creating a holy space to name and claim children. To "labor for peace" recognizes peace as a fundamental need and the only future for children. Practices of sanctuary confirm the mandate to shelter the most vulnerable when peacemaking efforts fail and when children need safety and resources for physical and spiritual growth. Finally, prayer depends on a posture of vulnerability—earnest desire, trust, and intense attention often best modeled by children. All four practices must engage children more directly than most people have understood.

One key priority shapes this book and guarantees its essential contribution not only to theological scholarship but also to the wider public: the value of children in and of themselves. This is both doctrinal conviction and moral mandate. Children are worthy not because they possess humility or charm or bring happiness or the reign of God but because they are created in God's image and elected by God. Children are already full persons "chosen" and "given to us." And "that gift demands our response." Thank you, David Jensen, for this clarion call.

—*Bonnie J. Miller-McLemore*

Preface

hildren challenge the work of Christian theology. Paying attention to the concrete circumstances of their lives transforms and enriches our understanding of the *imago Dei,* sin, and the church. More significantly, however, attending to children draws the church into practices of vulnerability and acts of care for children in the midst of the violence that threatens their lives. A theology of childhood considers children not for who they will become, but for whose they are and who they are. Theology that neglects children jeopardizes itself and imperils the lives of others, stopping its ears to the suffering of children across the globe, and in the end ignoring the child who lies at the center of Christian faith.

Two millennia ago, a baby was born in Bethlehem to an unwed teenage mother. Christian faith claims that a poor child embodies hope for the world, a Savior whose birth resembles the thousands of births that occur daily in slums and isolated villages throughout the world. If ever a child mattered theologically, surely Jesus did. Rarely, however, have Christians paid explicit theological attention to other children. Seldom has the child who inaugurated a reign of hope and peace been connected to the millions of children born subsequently in hopeless and violent circumstances. The point of this book is to address this neglect of childhood and children's lives, and to suggest that a renewed theological attention to the children in our midst hearkens the ground of Christian hope who comes as a child. Attending and caring for the children in our midst is an indispensable component of Christian discipleship, a component that demands fresh perspectives in the face of the multiple forms of violence that scar children today.

My intention in these pages is to offer an inductive theology of childhood that provides the basis of an ecclesial ethic of care for all children. The project is inductive, in the sense that it pays attention to concrete realities that imperil children's lives in the present age: war, poverty, child labor, the death penalty, and the sex trade, to name a few. Theology worthy of its name pays attention to particularity and context: I intend not to offer a blueprint of childhood from the outset that will be applied to children's lives indiscriminately; rather, I examine the differing shapes of childhood and the violence that threatens childhood in constructing theological portraits of children. An inductive theology begins with particularity and gradually steps toward more generalized statements about the nature of childhood. As much as possible, I strive to pay attention to children not in the abstract, but in their radical particularity. As I have written, the faces of the children I encounter daily have been constantly in view; perhaps this will occur for those who read this book as well.

Many works in psychology, history, and philosophy offer analogous attempts toward understanding childhood. Theology has much to learn from them, and I draw on several of these attempts in this book. Yet this work is a constructive theology, and differs from other interpretations of childhood insofar as it grounds its portrayal of children in the self-giving, self-disclosing God of covenant, incarnation, crucifixion, and resurrection. Another task of this work is to relate the claims made about childhood to the God who empties Godself in Christ for creation. The intent is not mere correlation, as if we could bolster our perception of children by invoking God; rather, the wisdom is more pointed: God is the God of all creation, and names children as God's own. To pay attention to this God is to pay attention to the faces of children who surround us.

Sallie McFague has written extensively on the need for advocacy theologies.[1] I consider the present book an attempt in that vein. In faithfulness to the crucified and risen Christ, an advocacy theology seeks to speak with those whose voices are often not heard. Children's voices often drown in the cacophony of commercialization and violence that characterize the (post)modern world. Attempting to hear them is fraught with peril: often we think we hear their voices when we really are hearing only ourselves and *our* intentions for children. A constant check on this work will be to portray as accurately as possible the realities of children's lives in multiple corners of the globe. Only by doing so can their voices be heard.

An advocacy theology, moreover, attends to the vulnerable in our midst. As a result, advocacy theologies are self-consciously ethical: they seek not only to describe patterns of graced life in God's world, but to promote attitudes and practices consistent with the proclamation of God's reign. An advocacy theology does not rest in describing the reign of peace, but calls for our participation in it. Such work invokes theology *and* ethics. Glimpsed one way, this book is a descriptive, constructive theology: by paying attention to children, we are better able to configure some basic claims of the Christian faith, including the *imago Dei,* church, and sin. Considered from another angle, however, this book recovers an ethic of care for the vulnerable children in our midst: a call for the church, in faithfulness to its Savior and proclamation of a reign of peace, to listen to children and become vulnerable for their sake. The result of such a work, however, is that it does not fit the tidy categories of systematic theology. Its subject matter, childhood, is relatively foreign to systematics and its presentation often drifts toward the genre of theological ethics. Some readers may find this approach frustrating. The *theological* account of childhood, however, gives the project coherence. Whatever suggestions I make about the church's posture toward children and the acts of care it is called to embody in the world draw their impetus from a descriptive account of childhood as vulnerability and difference in God's world.

An advocacy theology that claims to be Christian hearkens the voices of the vulnerable, broken, and downtrodden, because they claimed Jesus and he claimed them. Children constitute a disproportionate share of the world's downtrodden. One-third of the world's children live in abject poverty; more than a quarter of the world's children experience severe malnutrition; children are victims of the sex trade worldwide; in the United States, children may be executed for certain crimes.[2] In light of these pressing realities, it is no exaggeration to say that childhood itself is threatened in many quarters. An advocacy theology for children is not only an urgent response to these perils, but an exercise in faithfulness to the One who proclaimed children heirs to God's reign.

The greatest challenge in writing this work, however, has been the constant reminder that I am writing in some senses about what I am not. Though I argue in the end that childhood abides throughout human life, I am obviously no longer a child. As passionately as I argue for the church to hear children's voices, the voice in this book is not a child's. At first, this recognition seemed an impassible barrier for my own work, which almost caused me to relinquish the project. Can adults really speak about childhood? I have since come to embrace my difference in age and experience from a child's as further impetus for the work. If persons could only write about themselves in a narrowly construed sense, all writing would be tautological, and communication between persons would be reduced to a rather stilted "I" discourses. Such narrowly construed identity runs contrary to one of the hallmarks of Christian confession: communion. Christians profess a God who is communion (Trinity), a church of communion, a sacrament of Holy Communion, a Savior who is the communion of the human and the divine. No "I" exists in the Christian imagination without the Other. We are ourselves only in relation to others, and so we are summoned toward others, claimed, and changed by them. I speak in this work as an adult claimed by children, changed by them, and constantly in relation with them. The person I am cannot be reduced to a label of white, straight, Scandinavian-American father, but is continually shaped by my relations with radically different others.[3]

When theologians turn their attention toward children and are claimed by them, several doctrines are challenged, including our understanding of the human person, the *imago Dei,* sin, the church's ministry and sacramental life. The bulk of this work examines those challenges and the ethic of care toward children that they invoke. Chapter 1, "Consider the Children," offers a brief typology of the relative neglect children have received in various theological traditions. From the extreme of lamb-like innocence to total depravity, children have been romanticized and demonized with damaging results. Even the banal assumption that children are "adults in the making" has hampered an understanding of childhood as a locus of God's grace. Within these same traditions, however, are the whispers of alternative perspectives of children as partners in covenant and heirs to God's reign.

Chapter 2, "Fragments of Vulnerability and Difference," claims that to understand human relationality in the Christian tradition, one first looks to the pattern of God's vulnerable love for creation. The Christian story, broadly configured, centers on vulnerable love that embraces difference throughout creation: in covenant with an oppressed people, present in a vulnerable baby in Bethlehem, spilling out in Jesus' ministry of repentance, reconciliation, and proclamation of God's reign, incorporating the assault of human violence on a cross, and witnessed in love that goes beyond those spaces where we proclaim him as risen. This pattern of God's love for the world unveils the abundantly diverse forms of graced human life with God, and informs the nature of childhood.

Chapter 3, "The Vulnerable Child of God," strives to move beyond an essentialist anthropology that invariably excludes children as full bearers of the *imago Dei.* The center of my theological analysis explores childhood under the headings of vulnerability and difference. Children are chosen by God, open to relation with different others, pilgrims oriented to the present. Following this analysis, I turn my attention to dimensions present when children are nurtured: imagination, playfulness, and attentiveness, each of which are resonant with theological significance.

Chapter 4, "Vulnerability and Violence," turns to the tragic dimensions of childhood. Focusing on sin from the perspective of the "sinned against," this chapter exposes the multiple forms of violence inflicted on children worldwide: poverty, the sex trade, war, and child labor. In response to these perils, I argue for reconstructing the Christian doctrine of sin in ways that complexify our understanding of children as agents *and* victims of violence.

Chapter 5, "Practices of Vulnerability," steers toward ecclesiology. I explore four ecclesial practices—baptism, peacemaking, sanctuary, and prayer—that offer hope for children in the midst of consumer societies that celebrate acquisition and conquest. Chapter 6, "To Change and Become Like Children," closes by suggesting the possibilities and ambiguities of recovering human vulnerability in our age. Matthew's narration of "true greatness" with the example of the child (Matt. 18) provides the exegetical underpinning, while Karl Rahner's understanding of childhood as the basic condition that underlies graced human life offers a modern theological anchor. To be a child of God, I argue, is to become like children through God's grace, open to the joy of relation, but also susceptible to the tragedy and violence of human life in God's world. In response to the violence that threatens children's lives, the hope for their future rests in the possibilities of an alternative vision, epitomized in the gospel's unique privileging of children.

The result of this project, I hope, is a contextual theology that pays close attention to the blessing and peril of children's lives and upholds the care of children as one act of faithfulness to its crucified and risen Savior. I have become more convinced (and convicted) over the past several years that the most profound mysteries of the Christian faith are chimeras unless they touch the everyday. The incarnation, after all, claims that the mystery of God assumes ordinary human flesh. As disciples of the Incarnate One, theologians, too, must pay close attention to the everyday that God assumed: ordinary acts of care and community building, the divers vocations worthy of a life's work, the nurture of home, family, and friends. Caring for children is one of these ordinary activities that consumes years—yea, a lifetime—of joy, struggle, and pain.

It is high time we paid closer theological attention to it and to the children who are the subjects of our attention. I hope this book, therefore, will be read not only by professional theologians and parents, but by any person of faith called to ministries of care with children, since all of us, in one way or another, are bound together with generations younger than our own. Their well-being and our well-being go hand in hand.

This work, as all works of theology, will remain unfinished. As I have written it in snippets of time gathered between the everyday nurture of a marriage partnership and the labor of caring for our five-year-old daughter, I have no doubt that many of these reflections on childhood will change in the future as my daughter grows. There has never been a time when the book has received my undivided attention. As a result, this book is informed by my inadequate attempt to live out some aspects of the ethic of care for children that I point to throughout it. I know that I am a better theologian because I am a parent; I hope some dimension of being a parent has been enriched because of my work as a theologian.

In the middle of Nashville, Tennessee, a stone's throw from a glittering new professional football stadium, is one of the largest, most blighted housing projects in the city. Adjacent to those apartments is the Nancy Webb Kelly United Methodist Church's remarkable program, "Dare to Dream," which began as after-school tutoring and has now grown into an entire ministry of music, education, self-esteem, mentoring, and cultural appreciation for countless children. My three years of work with the children of Dare to Dream and its supervisor, Rev. Shirley Majors Jones, changed my life. They are my earliest inspiration for this work.

As the call to teach moved our family to Manchester College in Indiana, I drew deeply from the wells of Anabaptist-Pietist thought and practice. This sojourn with the Church of the Brethren taught me that peacemaking is indispensable to the life of Christian faith. I thank, in particular, Bob Bowman for his consistent sense of humor, guidance, and encouragement as I began to teach and explore in this new world, and for his example of a balanced life of parenting, scholarship, and ministry. Teaching at Manchester proved to me that one can care for children and teach without jeopardizing either calling, as long as one is not afraid to ask for help.

I now ply my vocation at Austin Presbyterian Theological Seminary, surrounded by colleagues who refuse to reduce each other to their scholarly and ecclesial labors. I am fortunate to work with friends who value children and recognize that this kind of workplace is rare, as is the trade that allows a man to be a father. Matthew Morse aided me with extensive bibliographic searches and saw this project off to an auspicious start. The students in my January 2003 course, "Christian Theology and Children," provided stimulating conversations, keen practical questions, and a wealth of personal experiences in addressing children theologically. Much of their influence is contained in the pages that follow.

Timothy Staveteig and Monitta Lowe at The Pilgrim Press offered encouragement for the project at critical junctures in writing. Grace Long read significant portions of the manuscript and gave incisive feedback. The Workgroup in Constructive Theology has shown me that *all* theology is collaborative. My own parents, John and Gretchen Jensen, lie in the foreground of these reflections on the nurture of children, and how it can be done with joy.

Hannah Grace Jensen, to whom this book is dedicated, has been present throughout the writing. Life has changed with her entrance into the world, and she has opened my heart to joy that defies the imagination. I could not write a book on childhood without including her on its pages.

Molly Hadley Jensen remains this book's greatest inspiration. She had confidence in it when I did not, and nurtured my own reflection through countless conversations. As both of us travel this path of parenting, writing, and teaching, it is reassuring to have a partner who shares in the laughter and pain of each step. Grace comes in partnership and in her daily embraces of care. I am thankful for the walk thus far and for all that is left to share.

I hope that the following pages contain some theological resources for calling the church's attention to children and the child who is the bearer of the world's hope. May what is helpful in that endeavor be retained and what is distracting from it be forgotten.

ONE

Consider the Children

hildren have rarely captured the sustained attention of Christian theologians. If children appear rather infrequently on the pages of theological classics, they have always lingered in their margins, beckoning the future, disrupting the undue seriousness of theological endeavor with play and laughter, crying out in protest when violence rends their lives. Theology's relative silence on children, however, does not overwhelm the voices of children even today. The Christian tradition, after all, places hope for the world in a child born to an unwed teenage mother in a Bethlehem stable. Children's voices demand to be heard, and occasionally in the history of Christian thought, some theologians have hearkened those voices and have even been changed by them. One task of this work is to hear those voices anew, and ask ourselves how the church might change if it is claimed by children.

Our forbears in the tradition have bequeathed us an ambiguous legacy on the topic of childhood. Intriguingly, no single doctrine of the child dominates throughout the centuries. Instead, we encounter widely variant themes throughout the ages, and the attempt to hold together conflicting tendencies in a general understanding of the human person. Over the centuries, Christians have maintained children as reflecting the burden of original sin par excellence and the blessing of God's future. Children, in this history, are both full recipients of God's covenant, and those who grow into those promises. In some cases, they have been considered fully human; in others, only marginally so. Blessing and burden, full members and partial members, children typically appear as theologians have grappled with other themes: baptism, the church, sin. In our conflicted history, they have been sources of hope and objects of abuse, subjects of attention and objects of neglect. Theological understandings of children *matter*, they have an impact, for good or for ill, on the way the church and society nurtures or neglects their unique lives. Who are children, and how are they reflections of the image of God? Some of the richest resources for addressing these questions appear rather early in the tradition.

CHILDREN OF THE COVENANT

Compared with many of the cultures of the ancient Mediterranean world, Israel valued and welcomed children wholeheartedly. At the center of Israel's regard of children was its understanding of covenant. Children, as inheritors of the covenant, did not grow into God's promises for the community, but were from birth participants in them. Though many consequences of the covenant were decidedly patriarchal (fathers wielded substantial authority over their children and any who cursed father or mother could be executed [Lev. 20:9]), generally speaking, the covenant regarded children as persons. They were not the mere objects of their parents' will, but the subjects of God's creative intent, a creativity that rendered each child unique and irreplaceable.

The signatory rite of this covenant was circumcision: "Throughout your generations every male among you shall be circumcised when he is eight days old, including the slave born in your house and the one bought with your money from any foreigner who is not of your offspring" (Gen. 17:12). Etched on each infant boy's body was a sign of the promise. The visible marker heralded the inclusion of the youngest in the fold, even those young (such as slave children) who might be considered "outsiders." Of course, the rite of circumcision, as presented in Genesis, is permeated with problematic assumptions: the physical sign is extended only to male children, the sign is imposed on the children of foreigners, and slavery is accepted as a given. Beneath these excruciating circumstances, however, lies an implicit embrace of children, signaled in a central liturgical act of the believing community. As the example of circumcision shows, the ritual practice of a community is a lens through which we might view that community's regard of children.[1] Judith Gundry-Volf summarizes this insight well: "Children were thus members of God's covenant with Israel . . . and it was expected that they would assume covenantal responsibilities."[2] Children stood not on the margins of covenant, but as participants in God's promises to Israel.

The familiar story of Israel's covenant-breaking and God's faithfulness to the covenant further documents the embrace of children. In the prophetic literature, children symbolize the dawning of a new day, when Zion will be restored, and the covenant will be engraved on people's hearts (Isa. 9:6; 11:6; Ezek. 37:25). Children epitomize hope for covenantal renewal. Isaiah expresses this hope succinctly: "My spirit that is upon you, and my words that I have put in your mouth, shall not depart out of your mouth, or out of the mouths of your children, or out of the mouths of your children's children, says the Lord, from now on and forever" (Isa. 59:21). Throughout the Hebrew Bible, children are seen as blessings for the future, signs of God's creative intent and faithfulness that surpasses all generations.[3]

Perhaps most significantly, however, Israel's regard of children as blessing was not restricted to the people of the covenant. Faithfulness to God's promises was expressed not only in welcoming Israel's children, but in an embrace of the vulnerable children of outsiders. "You shall not wrong or oppress a resident alien, for you were aliens in the land of Egypt. You shall not abuse any widow or orphan" (Exod. 22:21–22). As Israel heard the cries of the vulnerable children in its midst, it did not draw the line between children worthy of care and those who were not. All children, regardless of heritage, were blessings of God entrusted to the community's care. One test of Israel's faithfulness came in the person and witness of an orphan.[4]

According to the covenantal framework, children are valued not simply for their incipient adulthood, but for whose they are and who they are. Signs of God's blessing, hope for the future, and full members of the community, children are entrusted to communal care. In this sense, the covenant signals not a hierarchy of grace, but a promise extended to all Israel.[5] Though children grow into full covenantal responsibilities, they are already recipients of God's promises, and are themselves a blessing to the older generations.

SIN AND OBEDIENCE

If there is a leveling statement in the Christian tradition, it is surely the doctrine of original sin. In varying articulations, Christian faith claims that all persons are born into brokenness that precedes their arrivals on the scene. Human beings inherit the destructive consequences of these ruptures and reflect them in their daily lives; we are, moreover, responsible for the brokenness we create and in which we participate. No person, regardless of age, is exempt from sin's cancer. In some critical readings of original sin, the doctrine is ultimately pernicious in its effects: it blames infants before birth, implicates children in their own abuse, and suggests that children can only be tamed through injunctions to obedience and physical punishment. Biblical proof texts abound, particularly in the book of Proverbs: "Do not withhold discipline from your children; if you beat them with a rod, they will not die. If you beat them with the rod, you will save their lives from Sheol" (Prov. 23:13–14). According to this hackneyed understanding, sin is expressed most keenly in the folly of childhood and can only be tamed by a stern father and a disciplining God.[6] Though hardly a theologian in the tradition offers such a simplistic understanding of sin in relation to children, some tendencies within it lean in this direction.

Augustine displays some of these propensities. The early chapters of his *Confessions* read in places like a lament of youth. "Who can recall to

4

me the sins I committed as a baby? For in your sight no man is free
from sin, not even a child who has lived only one day on earth. . . . If I
was born in sin and guilt was with me already when my mother conceived me, where, I ask you, Lord, where or when was I, your servant,
ever innocent?"[7] Doubtless, Augustine's understanding of sin is complex and nuanced. Its effect is remarkably democratic, extending the
pallor of sin across all generations and attributing all righteousness to
God's grace. Yet at the same time, Augustine singles out young children
as prime examples of sin, even nursing infants who covetously wail at
the sight of another child at breast.[8]

The remedy, of course, for original sin is the unmerited grace that
God bestows. For some of the church fathers, the effects of grace led
toward greater obedience of one's earthly and heavenly Parent. John
Chrysostom, though admittedly more of an optimist on the question of
inherited guilt in infants,[9] implies that the proper relationship of parent
to child is profuse affection with the threat of physical force in cases of
youthful dalliance: "Have not recourse to blows constantly and accus-
tom him not to be trained by the rod; for if he feel it constantly as he is
being trained, he will learn to despise it. . . . Let him rather at all times
fear blows but not receive them."[10] By instilling obedience in children,
through a combination of affection and punishment, parents fulfill their
divine calling and contribute to the molding of children into fuller
members of the community. For Chrysostom and others in the early
church, the wayward tendencies of children demand reform.

Martin Luther echoes many of these reforming attitudes as well.
Though he did not claim that childhood itself was depraved,[11] he suggested that one of parents' roles was to tame children's stubbornness and
selfishness. "This work [of parenting] appears easy, yet few see it rightly.
For where the parents are truly godly and love their children not just in
human fashion, but (as they ought) instruct and direct them by words
and works to serve God in the first three commandments, then in these
cases the child's own will is *constantly broken*."[12] When parents broke
their child's will, they were instilling obedience not simply to themselves, but to God's word.[13]

Though none of these theologians equates childhood with the condition of sinfulness, each of them stresses tendencies of children that demand reform—at times under rather harsh measures. Each seems aware of ambiguities and tensions within childhood. Children are subjects of celebration and recipients of grace, yet also capable of selfishness and injury. The tendency in addressing this tension is to consider childhood as a state that will be molded into something more mature once the pernicious tendencies of children are stamped out. Childhood, then, serves partly as a foil to a life of mature discipleship, and is not celebrated for its own sake.

THE ANTITYPE: THE NATURAL CHILD

Dissenting voices within the tradition have often seized the doctrine of original sin as the prime example of Christian neglect of children. Many of these critics speak from beyond the structures of official theology and the church itself. The problem, for them, is not that children demand reform, but that society needs to return to its natural state. The source of sin is not children themselves, but in societies that corrupt children. According to this view, children are innocent; if left to themselves, if allowed to explore the world with gentle guidance, they will flourish beyond our imagination. Optimistic theories about children's nature permeated the Romantic movement and are fully manifest in Jean-Jacques Rousseau's *Émile*. This understanding of children might be considered the Christian antitype, since it distances itself from Augustinian anthropology and understandings of sin in an attempt to nurture children's lives.

For Rousseau, nature epitomizes the good: "Everything is good as it comes from the hands of the Author of Nature; but everything degenerates in the hands of man."[14] Children come into the world embodying the vigor of nature and the promise of the future. Hope lies in their escape from cities, "the graves of the human species,"[15] and the shelter of the countryside. Like many Romantics, Rousseau is unrestrainedly idyllic and decidedly anti-urban. In sentiments that have echoed in subsequent centuries, including the *New York Times* "Fresh Air Fund" and the Boy Scouts, the remedy for the pollution of urban society is to send children away to the forest.

Rousseau urges adults to let children be children: to play, explore, express their latent creativity. In returning to their natural state, moreover, children rely on themselves: "As for my pupil, or rather the pupil of Nature, early trained to rely on himself as much as possible, he is not in the habit of constantly resorting to others."[16] We do children a disservice if we teach them that corruption lies within; indeed, we instruct them to loathe themselves if this is the message they receive. Nature is the source of all good; our task in educating children is to allow them to reclaim their original nature and blessing.[17]

Ostensibly, Rousseau's educational philosophy calls for the celebration of childhood and the free development of each child. Beneath the surface, however, lie disturbing tendencies that echo the previous model on controlling and molding children. In his defense of rural education, Rousseau remarks: "In the village, a tutor will have much more control over the objects which he would present to the child. His reputation, his conversation, and his example will have an authority which they could not have in the city."[18] One is left wondering, in light of such statements, how much attention Rousseau lavishes on the tutor at the expense of children. Despite the rhetoric of freedom, Rousseau's regard of children seems conditional: The child is to resemble the tutor, and grow up in that model. When this model is afforded at all costs, it can be as tyrannical as a model that blames children for sin. Apparently, the polar opposite of original depravity may not be as sanguine toward the unique lives of children as it might first seem.

More problematic, however, is this model's inability to grapple with the reality of the brokenness that children, at times, are capable of creating. Innocence alone is too simplistic a read on children's lives. The reality of childhood is far more complex than this model (or the previous model) allows. Children are capable of boundless openness to the world and others, just as they are capable of injuring others. In the wake of Columbine and other acts of school violence, we have become painfully aware of this dimension of children's lives. Any attempt to interpret children must wrestle with the violence inflicted by their hands and which they experience to a far greater degree at the hands of adults.

GROWING INTO ADULTHOOD

Between the relative extremes of childhood as a personification of sin and the embodiment of innocence lies perhaps the most influential interpretation of children's lives: children are adults-in-the-making. In Western thought, this model has become widespread; Aristotle and other Greek philosophers accepted it, the legal system in the United States, in numerous ways, embodies it,[19] and it makes intuitive sense—children are not yet adults and are growing into their roles and responsibilities in society. A representative theologian who subscribes to this view is Thomas Aquinas, though, like each of the other theologians we have encountered, his views hardly fit neatly into any typology.

For Thomas, reason is one of the chief markers of a full life: the end of humanity is to worship, glorify, and contemplate God. Children, however, are not of an age where contemplation and the full use of rational capacities are possible. Speaking of infants and very young children, Thomas remarks: "So long as he has not the use of reason he is like a non-rational animal."[20] Though this comparison may strike the modern reader as unduly harsh and dismissive of children, it was meant to underscore the urgency and importance of caring for children. Because they do not have the capacity of reason, children are entrusted to parental and ecclesial care to guide them into fuller humanity. Having received this care, the child then develops free will and "begins to be his own master and to provide for himself in matters of divine and natural rights."[21]

Thomas's view of childhood renders the question of sin more complex. We can neither consider childhood the root of all rupture nor blithely announce it as primal innocence. Because sin, too, is connected to the misuse of our natural, rational capacities, children stand in unique relationship to sin. They, too, are inheritors of the guilt of original sin, but are not capable of manifesting the full scourge of its disastrous effects: "Before someone reaches the age of discretion, a lack of maturity impeding his use of reason excuses him from mortal sin, and so all the more from venial sin, should he do anything that is such objectively."[22] Distancing himself somewhat from Augustine's notion that young children were capable of manifesting willful activity that represented the rupture of sin, Thomas suggests that they cannot be culpable of sins of commission. Nevertheless, they are not innocent, since they are fully capable of sins of omission. They are guilty, as it were, of not turning the whole of their attention toward God: "A young person, beginning to have moral discretion, can, it is true, refrain for a while from other mortal sins, but he does not escape the sin of omission . . . unless he turns himself toward God as soon as he can."[23] Using reason as a marker, Thomas deftly avoids the harsh determinism that consigns infants to total depravity and hell, and the blithe optimism of innocence that ignores the pain that children are capable of inflicting on others.

The crux of his argument is the original *incompleteness* of the child. The child is the one who grows into the use of reason and proper worship of God, and thus grows into full personhood and accountability for sin. Childhood, in his view, is not an abiding reality, but a state that adults leave behind: "Childhood is not of the essence of being human and so the same person who was a child becomes an adult."[24] Thomas's account of children, though spotty, is actually quite sophisticated. It attempts to describe the development of the human person through different stages of God-given life. Each stage of life is blessed by God, but each stage is superseded by the next. Adulthood and the full use of reason constitute one end of human life, and childhood is valued because it leads toward that end. Insofar as his account grapples with the differences between the responsibilities and capacities of adults and children, it is laudable.

Yet his read of childhood is also plagued by inadequacies. Chief among them is the isolation of reason as a prime marker of humanity. Those who are not able to exhibit the full capacity of reason—not only infants and young children, but also the mentally ill, and persons with Alzheimer's disease—are accordingly, less than full human persons.

Thomas privileges a dimension of human life (the use of reason) at the expense of excluding others from participation in the fullness of human life. This isolation of reason is arbitrary (why reason as opposed to other dimensions of human life such as relationality or love?) and inattentive to the profound differences among human persons. Secondly, Thomas's account values children not so much for who they are but for who they will become. Children are on the way to personhood, and childhood is rapidly discarded along that way. Such an account runs the risk of ignoring the nature of childhood and the children in our midst. We encounter a possible alternative and patient attention to children in some of the gospels.

ATTENDING TO CHILDREN

The New Testament assumes much of the covenantal understanding of children that we explored earlier in this chapter. Yet, examples of children in the New Testament are sparing at best. On only a few occasions are children mentioned in the life of Jesus or as subjects of concern in the various epistles. For the writers of the New Testament, children did not occupy the center of attention. Yet amid this relative absence of attention are some suggestive encounters of Jesus with children that evoke attentive and caring responses toward children and the valuing of their lives in their own right.

The most familiar of these stories is Jesus' blessing of the children, a brief narrative recorded in each of the synoptic gospels (Mark 10:13–16; Matt. 19:13–15; Luke 18:15–17). When the disciples discourage children (Luke mentions infants as well) from approaching Jesus, he rebukes the disciples and invites children to come to him. And in the intimacy of human touch, he takes children in his arms, blesses them, and pronounces them heirs of God's reign.[25] This gesture, this rebuke of those who would send children away, is a summons to turn attention to children. This touch and blessing, moreover, is an extended metaphor of his own ministry: The Savior of the world touches those whom most would rather ignore, blessing and healing them for renewed life.

A surprising aspect of some gospel stories of Jesus with children is that children, at times, serve as models for adults. In Matthew 18, Jesus claims, "Unless you change and become like children, you will never enter the kingdom of heaven. Whoever becomes humble like this child is the greatest in the kingdom of heaven. Whoever welcomes one such child in my name welcomes me" (18:3–5). This inversion of status resonates with other strands of the gospel narratives, where the meek inherit the earth and the last are first. Since Matthew does not spell out what *becoming* like a child entails, Jesus' suggestion to the disciples has a cryptic ring. Nonetheless, he singles out the humility of children as cause for welcoming children: When the disciples welcome one humble child, they welcome Jesus. The unique face of each child summons our attention; in attending to children, we are opened anew to God's grace in the world.

The contrast with the Thomistic model here is obvious. Children are valued not for who they will become, but for who they are and whose they are. Yet we can romanticize these images of Jesus with children in the New Testament quite easily. His invitation to become like children can evoke nostalgia for a childhood devoid of responsibilities. Likewise, Jesus' summons to become humble can be stripped of its political content rather easily. Our society, it seems, is particularly adept at doing so. Typically, we idolize childhood and perhaps even long for it without paying attention to the vulnerable children in our midst. Jesus' invitation evokes the opposite response: to attend to the vulnerable and be changed by the pressing realities of children's lives.[26]

TOWARD A THEOLOGY OF CHILDHOOD

Amid these varying understandings of children in the Christian tradition, I believe the richest and most suggestive images stem from the first and last models: the covenantal framework of children as full members in the household of God and the whisper of an ethic of care implicit in the gospel narratives of Jesus with children. These depictions pay close attention to the circumstances of children's lives and value children for who they are. Indeed, they suggest that childhood is not a state that anticipates full human life, but an enduring reality saturated with meaning and grace.

In the pages that follow, however, I will suggest something more: Paying attention to children calls us to attend to children in care through practices of vulnerability. By becoming vulnerable with the children in our midst, we not only stake a claim with their lives, we also understand more fully what it means to be created in God's image and what it means to be church. The difference of each child lends light on the differently created creatures we are called to be. By paying attention to children's lives, which are threatened on many sides by the violence of war, poverty, the sex trade, and domestic abuse, the church offers its own distinctive practices—peacemaking, baptism, sanctuary, and prayer— that care for children in a broken world. These postures, moreover, remind us that the One whom we profess as Savior became vulnerable for our sake. In order to understand the distinctive nature of these practices and childhood itself, I turn first to some marks of God's vulnerability and the value of difference as witnessed in Christian tradition.

TWO   # Fragments of Vulnerability and Difference

hallmark of nearly every Christian understanding of the human person is that each person—regardless of mental capacity, physical stature, or social status—is uniquely created in God's image. Though the church's track record in translating this theological affirmation into practice continually falls short—witness its historical endorsement of slavery, the denial of women's full humanity, as well as its contemporary exclusion of gays and lesbians from ordained ministry—at the very least affirming the *imago Dei* implies the irreplaceable value of each child of God. Each one of us is unique, and creation itself groans if even one human being suffers. The God who is the ground and source of all that is reveals God's image not by impressing a uniform shape on all human lives, but in the staggering diversity of our differently shaped lives under God. The *imago Dei* is less an imprimatur for sameness than it is the grace that makes our differently shaped lives possible.[1]

The locus classicus for humankind in God's image is Genesis 1:26–27: "Then God said, 'Let us make humankind in our image, according to our likeness; and let them have dominion over the fish of the sea, and over the birds of the air, and over the cattle, and over all the wild animals of the earth, and over every creeping thing that creeps upon the earth.' So God created humankind in his image, in the image of God he created them; male and female he created them." Historically, many attempts to understand the *imago* have suggested an essence to human nature that all persons potentially share: rationality, power of dominion, morality, the capacity for love, or the possession of an eternal soul. Though each of these characteristics displays its own history of theological reflection, the biblical text is conspicuously silent in defining the *imago Dei*. Dominion—perhaps the most dominant thread of the story that theologians have emphasized—is not synonymous with the image of God and does not attribute God-like powers to human beings. Rather than emphasizing power, dominion locates human persons within the abundance of creation. Indeed, when Christians have equated dominion-as-power with the *imago*, they have narrowed their understanding of humanity with devastating results: a planet that now bears in every quarter the festering wounds of human rapaciousness. Such power begets not only ecological death, but also confutes the biblical narratives' depiction of the covenant-making, cruciform pattern of divine life.[2]

The image of God is not a mold that shapes human life in uniformity or establishes a common essence. Verse 27, which has received comparatively less attention than "dominion," reminds us as much: "in the image of God he created them; male and female he created them." God's image, in other words, is whispered in the *differences* of human persons. Genesis offers the example of sexual difference as one dimension, though there is no legitimate reason to restrict our understanding of difference to biological sex alone. Genesis 1 suggests that difference is writ large over the tapestry of creation: from the brilliance of the heavens, to the abounding vegetation of the earth, to the wriggling creatures that creep on the ground, life itself is possible because each living thing in God's creation is different from others. What scandal it is when we see human difference as the cause for exclusion, rather than inclusion in God's abundant life. This difference implies that vulnerability and openness to others are constitutive of human life in God's world, chords that we find echoed throughout scripture. The God of the Bible is not a monad enclosed upon itself, but a God who becomes vulnerable in relation to others, who calls us to live in vulnerability with others.

As this brief introduction has already shown, core theological convictions can bolster rather divergent responses: Glimpsed through a distorted lens, dominion evokes neglect and abuse of creation; seen in a more comprehensive light, dominion locates persons within a web of difference, caring for the different others with whom we are bound. Theology matters. The words we use for God, Christ, and creation shape not only our understanding of the mysteries of Christian faith, they inform our response to those mysteries. Theology is never separate from ethics. One cannot delineate the ontology of Christian faith apart from the reign of God that Jesus proclaimed. The task of this chapter, then, is to highlight a few fragments of God's vulnerability from the biblical narratives and explore their implications for how we understand human life in its abundant difference. If those narratives describe human persons as God's children, we must first anchor our reflections on childhood in an account of God's relationship with creation.

A GOD OF COVENANT

If we read the Hebrew Bible as a story, its pivotal and most interesting character is the God who creates and establishes a covenant with the people Israel. Whether the texts describe God's promises to Israel, the succession of judges and kings in the land, the wealth of wisdom gained from "fear of the Lord," or the prophetic denunciation of Israel's own oppression of persons in their midst, at the background of each text is a God who relentlessly seeks a people. The God of Abraham bears little resemblance to Aristotle's unmoved mover, who sits in supreme isolation, inaugurating the cosmic chain of events only to remain unaffected by anything God creates. Rather, the God of Hebrew Scripture sinks an anchor of vulnerability and relatedness in the world of creation. This is a God who makes promises to a particular people, who expresses anger when Israel lapses in its own faithfulness, who mourns when the people are lost, who remains with that people in all times, even in exile. Reading these narratives, we understand the God of Israel precisely as a God of relationship. "And I will walk among you, and will be your God, and you shall be my people" (Lev. 26:12). This is a God who chooses Israel, not because Israel is worthier than all others, but because of God's inexhaustible grace.

This covenant-making God is not impassible, unaffected by the mundane affairs of this world, but shows emotion, and even change of heart as covenant with Israel is established and renewed. Unlike the un-moved mover, the God of Israel is *supremely affected* by everything in creation. When Israel is indifferent to the covenant, God is the One who mourns. When Israel is oblivious to the oppressed in their midst, God reproaches the oppressors. The One who covenants with a people is nearer to that people than they are to themselves. In the words of Karl Barth, "In this divinely free volition and election, in this sovereign deci-sion (the ancients said, in His decree), God is *human*. . . . Thus He af-firms man. Thus He is concerned about him. Thus He stands up for him."[3] God enters into relationship with Israel not so much that God will thereby be complete (God as the Alpha and Omega is the well-spring of all fulfillment), but so that the people Israel may be fulfilled. Yet the promise of fulfillment also entails substantial risk: As Israel stumbles, breaks the law, and tramples on the oppressed, God suffers. By maintaining an intimate covenant with a particular people, the God of life reveals Godself in vulnerable relationship.

Covenant-making also implies a valuing of difference in the di-vine life. In a restless movement of grace, God chooses to relate to others who are *not God*. Despite the difference between the partners, the biblical narratives portray this relationship between God and Israel in quite intimate terms.[4] The divine life is not a mystery enclosed in itself, but embraces those who are not God. This scandal to the Greek mind is the ground of Christian hope: Words of God, that we are made for communion with God. If the God of covenant embraces difference, so too must we expect the shape of human life in God's image to be enormously varied.

A PREFERENCE FOR THE VULNERABLE

If the God of Abraham reveals Godself in covenant with a particular people, Israel's faithfulness to that covenant is reflected in its own embrace of the outsiders in its midst. The God who establishes a special relationship with a people also exhibits a preference for those on the fringes of the covenantal fold. Where Israel asserts its own privilege as the recipient of God's promise, God condemns Israel for not attending to the vulnerable. Indeed, covenant itself blurs the distinctions between insiders and outsiders.[5] God calls Israel to live as a covenant people by caring for the widow, orphan, and stranger.

Even the consummate outsider—the alien—according to Leviticus, lives as an insider: "When an alien resides with you in your land, you shall not oppress the alien. The alien who resides with you shall be to you as the citizen among you; you shall love the alien as yourself, for you were aliens in the land of Egypt: I am the Lord your God" (Lev. 19:33–34). In nearly every age, displaced people are the most vulnerable in society—witness the experiences of African slaves in the United States, Koreans in Japan, Kurds in Turkey. The temptation, of course, from the insiders' perspective is to draw the cultural lines rather tightly, to protect the ranks of the faithful and to exclude the stranger from even the most basic forms of hospitality. The alien is nothing less than a threat to my identity. The witness of Torah and the prophets, however, consistently subverts this tendency, and suggests that Israel's identity is bound up with the alien's. In the prophetic literature, denunciation of Israel's treatment of the poor and the alien occur mostly during times of heady economic prosperity: "Because you trample on the poor and take from them levies of grain, you have built houses of hewn stone, but you shall not live in them; you have planted pleasant vineyards, but you shall not drink their wine" (Amos 5:11). "Father and mother are treated with contempt in you; the alien residing with you suffers extortion; the orphan and the widow are wronged in you. You have despised my holy things, and profaned my Sabbaths" (Ezek. 22:7–8). Prosperity is a lie and covenant is broken when the alien and the poor live as outsiders in the land.

Another recurring test of Israel's faithfulness to the covenant is treatment of orphans. A more vulnerable character, indeed, is difficult to imagine, whether in our day or in the ancient Near East. The child alone, without a caregiver, has come to symbolize victimhood. Yet the biblical narratives refuse to reduce orphans—a contemporary analogue would be the street children of the world's cities—to mere symbols:

> When you reap your harvest in your field and forget a sheaf in the field, you shall not go back to get it; it shall be left for the alien, the orphan, and the widow, so that the Lord your God may bless you in all your undertakings. When you beat your olive trees, do not strip what is left; it shall be for the alien, the orphan, and the widow. When you gather the grapes of your vineyard, do not glean what is left; it shall be for the alien, the orphan, and the widow. Remember that you were a slave in the land of Egypt; therefore I am commanding you to do this. (Deut. 24:19–22)

The Hebrew Bible does not consider the orphan in abstraction from covenant, but offers a straightforward call to care for every orphan, every child in the streets. Because the orphan is a child of God, regardless of ethnic or religious heritage, s/he is the receiver of God's grace, and the recipient of Israel's attention. A theology of childhood, apparently, has deep covenantal roots.

The Old Testament narratives, however, do not belie an unambiguous preference for the vulnerable. The book of Joshua interprets the conquest of Canaan as a token of God's blessing. Such narratives do not easily correlate with the claim that God seeks out the vulnerable. Indeed, the voices of most vulnerable in these stories (the inhabitants of Jericho and Ai, whose children and women are slaughtered: see Joshua 6; 8:1–29; 10:28–43) are the very voices we do not hear. Though the Bible rarely pronounces an unambiguous blessing on military victory—military conquest is often superseded by subsequent faithlessness to the God who has protected Israel—the narratives' silence on the victims of battle suggests how easily vulnerability can become an excuse for elimination. Such textual ambiguity is present in the New Testament as well, particularly in the Book of Revelation, where the righteous are vindicated by the destruction of those who stand in righteousness' way. (See Rev. 17.) These texts cannot be harmonized with the others we have explored. As a result, they stand as question marks to any claim that God seeks vulnerability alone. Even in Jewish and Christian traditions that prize vulnerability as a mark of God's self-revelation, the logic of triumph can easily gain the upper hand.

The God who becomes vulnerable in relationship with Israel calls the covenant people to become vulnerable to those on the margins. Covenant does not curve in upon itself, reflecting Israel's special status before God, but radiates outward to include those whom Israel is most prone to reject—the alien, the orphan, the widow. The downtrodden become manifestations of Israel's faithlessness to the covenant, and calls for Israel to come home to God. Covenant privileges difference; just as God chooses to reveal Godself in the difference of a people God has chosen, that people keeps covenant in their embrace of different others. Stated alternatively, the "outsiders" summon the "insiders" to faithfulness and thereby become themselves "insiders" in the biblical drama. God's covenant with Israel is not for the confirmation of uniformity, but a mark of God's election of different others for intimate relation with God. Captured in the face of an orphan from another land, the covenant draws Israel toward care for all children, no matter how different they are.

THE BABE IN THE MANGER

The vulnerable God of the biblical narratives makes surprising choices: electing a displaced, enslaved people, bringing it out of slavery and into the promised land, only to choose those outside the covenantal fold as marks of Israel's faithfulness to their God. In contexts where power, might, and victory are prized, God's preference for the vulnerable is striking. This story of God's surprising self-revelation continues in the Christian understanding of the birth, ministry, crucifixion, and resurrection of Jesus. Turning first to the stories of Jesus' birth, God's vulnerability takes on distinctive flesh.

Only two of the gospels, Matthew and Luke, regard the infancy narratives to be important enough to include in the gospel proclamation. New Testament writings that pre-date Matthew and Luke, such as Paul's letters and the gospel of Mark, lack any mention of Jesus' birth or childhood. Apparently, then as now, one could proclaim the good news quite adequately without recourse to some miraculous account of Jesus' birth. To read the infancy stories, therefore, as proof of Jesus' messianic status (or of Mary's immaculate nature), is to invoke an ill-conceived apologetic. Yet, neither should we dismiss the birth narratives as second-generation accretions to the gospel message. They express something unique about the way in which a vulnerable God reveals Godself in overlooked spaces and people. The Christian story of incarnation begins not with glorious triumph, but in humility, homelessness, and in the pregnancy of an unwed, teenage mother.

Incarnation also echoes the strands of difference that abound in biblical narrative. God reveals Godself not in blazing theophany or alienating antithesis to humanity, but in our flesh. The lynchpin of Christian revelation is that God becomes human, the Son of God who is Word of God. God chooses the difference of a human being for intimate relation. To paraphrase Chalcedon, in Christ God and humanity are united without division, without confusion, without separation. The divine life seeks otherness. God's incarnation in Christ does not obliterate the distinctions between human and divine nature, nor does it render a tertium quid; in Christ, the divine and human nature are preserved and kept distinct, but only in communion with each other. Jesus Christ is the enfleshment of communion-in-difference, and God's promise of that communion with us.

Though the Lucan and Matthean versions of Jesus' birth differ markedly in detail, characters, and resolution, they both emphasize some of the scandalous circumstances that surround it. From the very beginning of Matthew's account, questions of Jesus' illegitimacy swirl: "When his mother Mary had been engaged to Joseph, but before they lived together, she was found to be with child from the Holy Spirit. Her husband Joseph, being a righteous man and unwilling to expose her to public disgrace, planned to dismiss her quietly" (Matt. 1:18b–19). To all appearances, this pregnancy was a scandal. Matthew appears pained by this, and yet his account of Joseph's initial plan strikes the reader as doubly tragic and shamelessly patriarchal: Though professing to be unwilling to expose Mary to "public disgrace," Joseph most likely had his own reputation in mind as well, as he planned to "dismiss her quietly." Where, might we ask, would a pregnant teenage girl go? The scandalous circumstances of Mary's pregnancy nearly give birth to even greater tragedy. Though Joseph is shown in a dream to remain with Mary (v. 20), the story of Jesus begins with a stigmatized mother and an adoptive father concerned with reputation. The baby Jesus comes into the world not to ignore the stigma of the vulnerable, but to enflesh it.

Luke's gospel records the marginality of Jesus' birthplace. In words that have become the trappings of innumerable Christmas crèches, the story rarely evokes the danger and poverty of his birth. "And she gave birth to her firstborn son and wrapped him in bands of cloth, and laid him in a manger, because there was no place for them in the inn" (Luke 2:7). The One who comes in the name of the Lord comes into the world on a pile of hay, amid the smell of livestock and manure. This Son of God comes not in clouds of glory, but as a destitute infant, utterly dependent on his mother for every morsel that gives him life. Christian hope comes in a poor child, for whom there is no room in respectable quarters. Jesus' birth, like those in the world's poorest nations, is full of the promise of new life, yet also threatened by the forces of power and privilege that prey on the vulnerable. It is no small miracle that Jesus survives.

Indeed, as Matthew records the story, Jesus is marked for murder by one of these powers: the jealous Herod, whose wrath devours the innocent. "When Herod saw that he had been tricked by the wise men, he was infuriated, and he sent and killed all the children in and around Bethlehem who were two years old or under, according to the time that he had learned from the wise men" (Matt. 2:16). Though the gospel records the escape of Mary, Joseph, and Jesus, it does so without words of elation. Rather, it juxtaposes the family's escape with a stark account of the massacre of young children in Bethlehem who die at the hands of power gone mad. As the vulnerable God is revealed in a baby, the powers-that-be cannot bear it, and resort to senseless slaughter.

From its commencement, the story of Jesus summons the reader's attention to the vulnerable. His nativity evokes solidarity with the thousands of children born amid violence and poverty. His escape to Egypt occurs as other children are killed. This birth both exposes the horrors that seem to defy hope, and promises that violence will not have the final word. Jesus' birth anticipates his proclamation of God's reign, naming the powers that enslave and murder, pointing to a different order where power is made manifest in reconciliation and vulnerability. His story, in short, does not claim us until we are caught up in the reign that Christ proclaims. From the beginning, this story is about a "kingdom ethics," a summons of care for the children in our midst.

JESUS AMONG THE VULNERABLE

As Jesus increases "in wisdom and stature" (Luke 2:52, RSV), he embarks on a ministry marked by its own preference for the vulnerable. The Savior, who comes to the world as a child, directs our attention not chiefly to himself, but to others. Incarnation, in this sense, enfleshes a reign where vulnerability and difference are not marks of exclusion, but of relationship with God. Though unpacking his historical ministry is fraught with difficulty, the gospels emphasize at least three critical aspects that call our attention to the marginalized: 1) his healing of the ostracized; 2) his table-fellowship with the despised; and 3) his proclamation of the reign of God.[6]

In a society that ostracizes lepers because of their disease, Jesus ignores the barriers erected against them. Jesus, in other words, is a transgressive healer, disregarding the societal codes that would consign lepers to a fringe existence. He is the one who touches the untouchables and heals them not simply of a physical ailment, but restores them to fuller communion with others. In John Dominic Crossan's words, "By healing the illness . . . Jesus acted as an alternative boundary keeper in a way subversive to the established procedures of his society."[7] Jesus pays attention to and heals those whom others pretend do not exist (Luke 17:11–19; Matt. 8:1–4).[8]

On multiple occasions, Jesus heals children: he restores a girl to life (Mark 5:35–43); he drives an unclean spirit from a young boy (Mark 9:14–29); he exorcizes a demon from a young girl (Mark 7:24–30); and he heals an official's son (John 4:46–54). Jesus pays close attention to the plight of children, to those who in many cases bear the brunt of the world's injustice and disease.[9] Though each of these incidents merits a theological analysis of its own, the pericope of Mark 5:35–43 offers details that are particularly significant as Jesus embraces the children in his midst. Jarius, one of the leaders of the synagogue, has just reported his daughter's death. When Jesus, Peter, James, and John come to Jarius's house, they encounter a commotion of "people weeping and wailing loudly" (v. 38). Then as now, the loss of a child is utterly disruptive to the order of human life: a premature end to a life full of promise, a tear in the fabric of the human family. When a child dies, the loss is not only devastating to the parents, who will never fill the void now present in their lives, but to the larger community as well. With the death of a child, that community's future is wounded, a dimension of its hope for tomorrow is lost forever. Parents will never again hold their daughter's hand, their son will never gaze into their eyes and ask them the questions that all children ask. The beauty of that child's face will now only be preserved in the parent's and the community's memories, close to the heart, perhaps, but never as intimate as when we gaze at each other face-to-face. No wonder that the only response among the living is to weep and wail.

Jesus comes into this scene and makes a puzzling claim: "Why do you make a commotion and weep? The child is not dead but sleeping" (v. 39). At first, it appears that Jesus is oblivious to the tragedy that has just befallen the community. What seems initially to be obliviousness, however, proves anticipatory of the life and healing that only Jesus can bestow. Jesus' response is arresting: Instead of a hurried and hollow words of God's presence in the girl's death, Jesus touches and heals both the girl who has been lost and the crowd that grieves. Jesus ministers instead of offering a theological explanation. In a powerful model for the shape of ministry, he attends to the lives and the pain in his midst rather than distancing himself from it through pious words. The daughter who was lost to death lives again when Jesus takes her by the hand. Jesus goes into the house, touches the hand that her parents believe they will never hold again, and tells the girl to get up. This dynamic of Jesus touching, naming, and calling out to those beyond the pale—either through illness, ostracism, or death—repeats itself over and again throughout the gospels. He touches those whom others will not touch—children and adults— and restores the dead and despised to abundant life in God's world.

Jesus' practice of table fellowship further enfleshes the Savior's solidarity with the vulnerable. Sharing a meal is perhaps the basic gesture of hospitality: to break bread and pour wine with another person is not simply to share sustenance, but to share oneself and be changed by another. When Jesus breaks bread, the customary rules of acceptable table fellowship change: Jesus will dine with *anybody*, and even invites himself to another's table (Zacchaeus, Luke 19:1–10). The One with bread in his hand and wine in his cup will share company and feed anyone who is hungry, alienated, or lonely; those who are fed, in turn, feed Jesus. The meals that Jesus shares become parables for his whole life, extensions of himself for a world hungry and in pain, where bodies long for healing and wholeness. In a ministry marked by the most basic acts that sustain human bodies—healing and feeding—Jesus invites the vulnerable and wounded to find rest in him, while he rests with them.

The actions of Jesus' ministry find further resonance in his own proclamation of the *basilea*. Jesus' preaching of God's reign centers not on another place, but on a reorientation of *this world,* where children hold prominent place: "Let the little children come to me; do not stop them; for it is to such as these that the kingdom of God belongs" (Mark 10:14b). To proclaim the reign of God is to see the world through children's eyes, in which all human persons are recipients of God's grace, in which all persons are valued simply because they are. Through his actions of healing and reconciliation, Jesus inaugurates an alternative way of living: away from the structures that divide, enslave, and block our attention to God; toward each other not because we are essentially the same, but because we embody difference that is fundamental to relation with each other and with God. The reign of God is Jesus' proclamation of the reality embodied in his person, a life expressed in its unwavering orientation to God and different others.

THE VULNERABILITY OF THE CROSS

Jesus' focus on others, however, is the very orientation that the world cannot bear. The One whose life bears the marks of God's vulnerability for us is the very One who is crucified by the Roman Empire. Countless strands in the theological tradition have rightly turned our attention to the cross as a moment of decisive and enduring significance, yet the risk in this cross-ward turn is that Golgotha alone is the pivot upon which the world turns. Anselm's influential *Cur Deus Homo* veers toward this valorization of suffering. Undoubtedly rich in its probing of the nature of human sin, God's righteousness, and the goodness of creation, *Cur Deus Homo* emphasizes the freely given, albeit necessary, atoning death of Christ on the cross. In his analysis, humanity's debt to God, for sin, is infinitely serious: "Thus man is inexcusable, because he willingly incurred the debt, which he cannot pay, and by his own fault involved himself in this inability, so that he can pay neither what he owed before sin . . . nor what he owes on account of sin."[10] This infinite debt can only be satisfied by the voluntary self-giving of the sinless God-man: "Nor can a man give himself more fully to God than he does when he surrenders himself to death for His honor."[11] Christ's death thus becomes the keystone that bridges the entire redemptive order, without which humankind is lost, without which the demands of God's justice remain forever unsatisfied.

What is most striking in hindsight, is Anselm's relative inattention to the life and ministry of Jesus throughout his essay. Jesus' proclamation of the reign of God, his practice of table-fellowship and healing disappear into the background, or appear only as preludes to the cross. In a sprint to Golgotha, the vulnerability of the Savior and those in his midst slowly fade from view.

Instead of glimpsing the cross as the consequence of God's relentless demand for justice, might we better view it as the tragedy of a Savior who becomes vulnerable for the world? Jesus of Nazareth is the One whom the violence and power of the world cannot bear. The demands of God's justice, in the end, are not what cause the crucifixion; rather, it is the world's unwillingness to embark on the path of vulnerable discipleship that Jesus has unveiled. Closing our eyes to others, we reject him and his way and let the Empire annihilate him. The cross thus becomes not a cipher for God's justice, but a symbol of the tragedy of the vulnerable Savior and our sin. The violence of the cross does not originate in the life of a God who demands satisfaction, but in creatures bent on their own sense of power and privilege. Marking God's incorporation of tragedy, suffering, and death into God's very self, the cross is initially a symbol of anguish, and only subsequently a symbol of triumph. Few theologians of any age have recognized this tragic dimension of the cross as much as G. W. F. Hegel. For Hegel, God's identification with humanity is so strong that God will undergo the most humiliating death to exist in solidarity with God's creation: "God has died, God is dead—this is the most frightful of thoughts, that everything eternal and true is not, that negation itself is found in God."[12] A theology of the cross, in other words, does not rest content with a depiction of God's justice being satisfied by a Son's self-giving death; rather, it probes more deeply the tragedy of that death, by seeing it as a moment in the God who gives life. This is a God who does not remain distant from the suffering of the world, but takes it as God's own. Only thus is suffering seen in its appropriate light: not as a necessity that placates a God obsessed with order, but as a tragedy that God takes into Godself and even transforms into life. God hangs on the cross, in other words, and takes up all crosses, but does not allow them the final word.

William Placher has suggested that this odd dynamic of the gospels —its consistent inversion of power—reveals the heart of the story and offers a foretaste of what being human looks like when oriented to God:

> As the story progresses, Jesus becomes more and more power-less, less and less free—able perhaps to raise a following in Galilee, still with a chance to escape in the garden, then a bound prisoner, nailed to a cross. Yet the telling of the story implies an odd inverse proportion, for that moment when it seems that Jesus can do nothing at all is the culmination of his work as savior of the world. . . . In this story Jesus shows what it is to be most human, most like what a human being is supposed to be, living in full obedience to God.[13]

The strange good news of the Christian story is that the cycle of power, privilege, and violence are ultimately empty; the God of this story exhibits a preferential option for vulnerability and powerlessness, thus revealing Godself as the source and power of life itself. Only a crucified God can unmask the idols of power for what they really are: idols that obscure, inhibit, and destroy the abundance of life under God.

CHRIST RISEN

Of course, to claim Jesus as the Christ is not to leave him hanging on the cross. Good Friday does not pronounce the final word of the good news. "If there is no resurrection of the dead, then Christ has not been raised; and if Christ has not been raised, then our proclamation has been in vain and your faith has been in vain" (1 Cor. 15:13–14). God takes the anguish, humiliation, and death of Jesus and raises the Son from the grave. The temptation of any resurrection proclamation is to wax eloquent on the triumph over death and the grave and to minimize the time between Good Friday and Easter, when Jesus lay dead in the tomb. The church, generally speaking, has ignored Holy Saturday.[14] Cross, the tomb, and resurrection are each elements of the surprising good news of the Christian story, which we anesthetize if we neglect any one element of it. Christ's resurrection cannot be reduced to the glib slogan that death and suffering reign no more; rather, it suggests that despite all evidence to the contrary, the God of Jesus is a God of life, a God who incorporates the world's pain into God's very being. One dimension of the resurrection good news is that the lives of the dead continue to speak. It empowers the church never to forget the saints who have preceded us. As Johann Baptist Metz has written: "A Christian soteriology cannot be a casuistic cover-up for real suffering. . . . Above all, the silent suffering of the in-consolable pain of the past, the suffering of the dead continues, for the greater freedom of future generations does not justify the past sufferings nor does it render them free."[15] In a milieu that esteems the history of the powerful and suppresses the victims of power—celebrating European in-genuity in the New World while ignoring the annihilation of indigenous peoples and cultures—the good news is that no story is forgotten. Those who die live in the light of Christ's resurrection, which does not extin-guish the past, but illumines it, drawing the past—in all of its ambiguity, tragedy, and pain—toward its fulfillment in God's very life.

In Christ's resurrection from the dead, God takes the voices of the dead as God's own. This is the vulnerability of resurrection, that God does not erase death, but undergoes death to carry the voices of history's victims beyond the grave. God becomes vulnerable in the anguish of suffering and death, and by summoning those voices pro-claims that communion with God endures after death. Resurrection hope is not a palliative, but God's expression of solidarity with a world rent by violence, an anticipation of a peaceable reign that only God can bring.

What is perhaps most interesting about the New Testament ac-counts of the Risen Christ's appearance is that the disciples *rarely* recog-nize him on first glance. Jesus comes to them as risen, and his followers see him not. Only when he partakes in actions that evoke his ministry, are their eyes opened: in the breaking of the bread, in calling them by name (Luke 24:13–35; John 20:11–18). His presence among them is not one that can be readily identified or reduced to the confines of the familiar. Rather, his presence draws them outward: recalling the vulnerable of his own ministry, the Risen Christ invites us to encounter and be claimed by them.[16] As Mark's terse narration proclaims, "Do not be alarmed; you are looking for Jesus of Nazareth, who was crucified. He has been raised; he is not here. Look, there is the place they laid him. But go, tell his disciples and Peter that he is going ahead of you to Galilee; there you will see him, just as he told you" (16:6–7). The Risen Christ is the One who goes ahead of us, returning to the birthplace of his ministry. He does not remain closed unto himself, but seeks others to follow him. Difference, once again, is fundamental to proclaiming and following Jesus Christ. To proclaim him as risen is to be drawn toward Galilee, where Jewish and Gentile worlds intersect.

THE TRIUNE GOD

The most distinctively Christian affirmation about God is its stress on God's triune life. God is both constituted by an eternal, internal relationship of three persons—Father, Son, and Holy Spirit—and relates externally to creation in an analogous manner.[17] God is not an isolated monad who relates distantly and tangentially to creation, but gives God's very self, creating, sustaining, redeeming, loving. In the beginning, written into the very nature of God is relationship. Christians affirm God as triune and God's relationship to creation as triune because the Christian story (in its scriptures and ongoing experiences of life in the world) points to the life-endowing activity of the Creator, the redeeming work of Christ, and the renewing activity of the Holy Spirit —none of which are ever separate from one another, none of which is reducible to the other. Christians come to know God as triune because of the renewing activity of the Holy Spirit, the redeeming work of Christ, the life-inaugurating work of the Creator. Trinitarian theology is rooted not in abstruse speculation, but in the ongoing life, experience, and worship of the Christian Church.

The Trinity gives voice to the intensely communal, relational substructure of Christian faith. That faith posits not simply our external relation to God, but *participation* in God's very life. With words that sound blasphemous to Hellenists, Christians construe the community's prayer, worship, and praise taking place *within God*. Christians participate in God because the very nature of God's life is communion-in-difference, a God who is constituted by a relationship of persons, who extends that life graciously to others. As S. Mark Heim has written, person, not essence, is the "most basic category of the triune God. . . . To be and be in relation are the same thing for the divine life."[18] Communion occupies a central place in the Christian understanding of the world: salvation as eternal communion with God, church as the communion of believers, grounded in the God who is a communion of distinct persons.

Trinitarian faith claims that *difference and otherness* are fundamental to the divine life. God, for Christians, is not a fount of uniformity who transforms others into God's identity by divine fiat, but a God who establishes relationships with others in self-giving love. The being of God is communion-in-difference that seeks different others. Eastern articulations of the Trinity have tended to emphasize the difference intrinsic to God more than Christians in the West, through the symbol of *perichoresis*: the mutual self-giving, inhering, eternal dance between Father, Son, and Holy Spirit. The persons of the Trinity "*are what they are* only in relationship to each other. Each exists only in this relationship and would not exist apart from it. Father, Son, and Holy Spirit live only in and with and through each other, eternally united in mutual love and shared purpose."[19] Just as God is internally related, God seeks out creation, so that this other might be. The triune God gifts creation into being by birthing it into intimate relationship. In giving birth to us, God, our Mother, undergoes vulnerability for our sake. The Trinity thus symbolizes God's interaction with others that are enfleshed throughout the Christian story: A God who restlessly seeks others and becomes vulnerable in that process: birthing, sustaining, covenanting, redeeming. The Triune God is a God of vulnerable love made real in the flesh.

The communion that Christian faith envisages is not possible without difference—a difference that extends to the eternity of God's very life. The Trinity is thus both a theological claim that roots Christian faith in the ongoing activity of Creator, Christ, and Holy Spirit, and an ethical foundation for valuing and celebrating the difference of creation. Faithfulness to the Triune God entails an embrace of difference, not eschewing it as scandal. As Heim writes, "In the divine-human communion that is salvation, the *difference* between humanity and God is not the primary obstacle to religious fulfillment, but a necessary prerequisite to the deepest relation with God, one that recapitulates God's own mode of relation."[20] Just as God's life is communion-in-difference, human life in God's image is not possible without the radical difference each child brings to the world.

IN GOD'S IMAGE?

At the beginning of this chapter, I glossed the multiple ways in which Christians have understood humankind in God's image. Many of the interpretations of the *imago Dei,* unfortunately, have suggested that human beings reflect, or possess, a quality that distinguishes human creatures from the rest of God's creation: human rationality that facilitates contemplation of God, human power that engenders dominion over other creatures, human morality that distinguishes us from the rest of the animal kingdom. The problems with identifying the *imago Dei* with a quality, however, are manifold: it raises the question of human beings whose rationality or moral facility may not fit supposed norms, such as infants, the mentally ill, and persons with Alzheimer's disease. Are human beings who do not sufficiently exhibit the supposed quality that signifies the *imago Dei* to be considered "less human?" Though we may shudder at this thought, strands within the tradition, at times, have suggested as much. Consider one theological defense of slavery: "It is quite possible that [God's] favor may now be found with one class of men, who are holding another in bondage. Be that as it may, God decreed slavery—and shows in that decree, tokens of good-will to the master."[21] Any schema that betokens a hierarchy of divine gifts that some partake in lavishly while others lack them has no place in Christian theology. Distilling the *imago Dei* to a human quality inevitably leads us to consider some (usually ourselves) more fully human than others; it places the self at the center of the universe and victimizes those who are different.

I would join the chorus of a growing number of Christian theologians who see the *imago Dei* less as some common essence that all human beings share than the differently shaped relationships into which we are born. One dimension of the *imago Dei* is human vulnerability and difference, constituted in relation to God and relation to each different human other. Christians understand relationship by participating in the relation that grounds all relations: the Triune God of creation, incarnation, crucifixion, and resurrection. God, for whom otherness is constitutive of life, gifts human beings into relationship with God and with each other. Yet, as we have seen from this chapter, the relational God of the Bible is also a God of vulnerability. As William Placher has written, "To read the biblical narratives is to encounter a God who is, first of all, love (1 John 4:8). Love involves a willingness to put oneself at risk, and God is in fact vulnerable in love, vulnerable even to great suffering."[22] Relationality is both the promise and peril of human existence: opening us to the bedazzling difference of creation itself and the possibility that we may abuse and objectify the others with whom we are called.

Children are vivid reminders of the gift of difference that human persons embody. Each child is unique; each child comes into the world utterly dependent on others for biological survival and subsequent growth. Without relationship, children die. Children are born into a world fraught with the promise of gifted life with others and the peril that others may victimize and prey upon them. Children enflesh and help clarify some of the Christian understanding of the *imago Dei*. They do not encapsulate the *imago,* nor do they reflect it unambiguously. Yet very few theological understandings of the *imago Dei* have focused on children, and the promise and peril that their lives entail. Such is the intent of this experiment in theological advocacy: to approach childhood from a theological perspective, to understand childhood as one dimension of the vulnerable, related existence into which human beings are called, and to draw some implications of how a renewed attention to children impels us to reconfigure some pivotal practices in the church and to become vulnerable ourselves in those very places where children's lives are most seriously threatened. Recalling the basic theological convictions just outlined, I now turn to a more focused discussion of the theological dimensions of childhood.

THREE

The Vulnerable Child of God

f Christians understand the *imago Dei* less as a common essence that all persons share, and more as the vulnerable difference-in-relation that makes human life possible, then we should expect the shapes of human life under God to be enormously varied. The God who creates human persons in the divine image does not impose a mold of conformity that outlines terrestrial life; rather, God creates children who embody the differences that are prerequisites to relationship. If the Trinity suggests that difference is fundamental to the life of God, creation also bears witness to the difference that is the pulse of cosmic existence. God and creation relentlessly seek otherness. The God who creates in love does not remain enclosed upon Godself, but lets others be, to be in relation. Creation itself is marked by the abundant difference of creation and points to the difference that is God's life. Otherwise, relation would be solipsistic. Though human sin has warped the *imago Dei* and taught us to see difference as a scandal (if only "they"

were more like "us"), the graced shape of human life will always bear the marks of difference that are fundamental to the life of God and the cosmos itself. Created in God's image, we are called not simply to tolerate human difference, but to embrace it and recognize difference for what it is: the life of our bodies together in God's world.

When we turn to the lives of children, these differences strike us anew. Each child who comes into the world is the bearer of a unique personal history—the circumstances of her birth, his cultural heritage, the scarcity or abundance of nourishment in infancy—and as a metaphor of hope for the future.[1] Even in the direst of circumstances, the birth of a child can bring with it at least the *hope* for a better life. One of the enduring tragedies of life in our era is that hope for most children on the planet is rather short-lived. Beset by war, famine, disease, sexual exploitation, and hard labor, children themselves are endangered species in all quarters of the world, including North America. Though we will examine the multiple strands that threaten children's lives in the next chapter, it is important that we acknowledge them from the outset. For the vast majority of the world's children, childhood itself—as the space and time in which we claim God's choice of us, pay attention, imagine, and play—exists in name only.

What does it mean to be a child? Does childhood suggest something unique about the God who creates in love, who creates us differently? Such questions resist easy answers. This chapter will not attempt to offer any. Instead, it will suggest an approach to a better theological understanding of childhood by focusing on some biblical narratives that underscore children's vulnerabilities and that call attention to the vulnerability that human life entails. I begin by looking at two "marginal" characters of the Hebrew Bible—Ishmael and Hagar—and suggest that the narrative points to childhood vulnerability and childhood chosenness. Continuing with more explicit theological reflections on difference, election, and pilgrimage, I turn to an example from the gospels of Jesus' connection of the reign of God to the lives of children. Finally, I explore three dimensions of childhood vulnerability, crucial to a fuller understanding and celebration of the human person: imagination, paying attention, and playfulness.

Though such dimensions are often dismissed as traits that children outgrow, I argue that they are fundamental to abundant human life. The chapter closes by arguing that a theological reconsideration of childhood can reorient human life, in eros for the other and for God.

A MOTHER AND CHILD ON THE MARGINS

But Sarah saw the son of Hagar the Egyptian, whom she had borne to Abraham, playing with her son Isaac. So she said to Abraham, "Cast out this slave woman with her son; for the son of this slave woman shall not inherit along with my son Isaac." The matter was very distressing to Abraham on account of his son. But God said to Abraham, "Do not be distressed because of the boy and because of your slave woman; whatever Sarah says to you, do as she tells you, for it is through Isaac that offspring shall be named for you. As for the son of the slave woman, I will make a nation of him also, because he is your offspring." So Abraham rose early in the morning, and took bread and a skin of water, and gave it to Hagar, putting it on her shoulder, along with the child, and sent her away. And she departed, and wandered about in the wilderness of Beer-sheba.

When the water in the skin was gone, she cast the child under one of the bushes. Then she went and sat down opposite him a good way off, about the distance of a bowshot; for she said, "Do not let me look on the death of the child." And as she sat opposite him, she lifted up her voice and wept. And God heard the voice of the boy; and the angel of God called to Hagar from heaven, and said to her, "What troubles you, Hagar? Do not be afraid; for God has heard the voice of the boy where he is. Come, lift up the boy and hold him fast with your hand, for I will make a great nation of him." Then God opened her eyes and she saw a well of water. She went, and filled the skin with water, and gave the boy a drink.

God was with the boy, and he grew up; he lived in the wilderness, and became an expert with the bow. (Gen. 21: 9–20)

The story of Abraham, Sarah, and Isaac — who form a triumvirate of covenant—tends to be straightforward for most exegetes. Though their story is riven with jealousy, the looming specter of child sacrifice (Gen. 22), and the frailty of sin, at the very least the drama of these three characters offers a glimpse at some of God's promises to God's people. The story of Abraham, Hagar, and Ishmael has proven more challenging. Occupying far less space in the biblical narratives than the "mainline" characters, Hagar and Ishmael appear at the margins of social respectability and on the fringes of God's covenant. Their story, at first glance, appears more a narrative of exclusion than one of promise. Small wonder that the story of the slave and her son has captured far less attention over the centuries than that of the more "respectable" members of family. In Genesis 21, Ishmael is not even named. He is significant only insofar as he is connected to Abraham, and this connection is somewhat tenuous, given his status as the child of a slave. Yet, upon closer examination, the vulnerabilities that mark the life of the child and his mother give way to God's embrace of them. This child of exclusion is also a child of promise, one chosen by God. Though Sarah's machinations and Abraham's banishment of the two to the wilderness nearly lead to Ishmael's and Hagar's death, mother and child find refuge in the wilderness and therein an echo of God's call.

Their story, however, does not begin auspiciously. Ishmael is the child of a rape. Sarah's barrenness becomes the thin excuse for her giving Hagar "to her husband Abram as a wife" (Gen 16:3b). Hagar has no voice in the matter; in a story that repeats itself hauntingly throughout the centuries, resisting the master would prove futile. Hagar eventually gives birth to Ishmael and in the subsequent turn of events, Sarah's tainted "gift" becomes the locus of her own jealousy. Unable to bear the sight of the child of the slave playing with her own child, Sarah commands her husband to banish Ishmael and Hagar to the wilderness. Laden only with bread and a skin of water, the two leave home and are soon faced with starvation and death.

The portrayal of Sarah here is troubling: Though present as an indispensable part of the covenantal drama, she is also a conniving schemer. Perhaps her cunningness is the result of her own limited power in a patriarchal drama; perhaps it is the result of the biased hand of a patriarchal author. Regardless, however, her response is to assert whatever authority she has to exclude those who stand "under" her power. Both Sarah and Abraham, in this regard, are tragic figures, who construe difference as cause for exclusion and banishment.

At this point, it is tempting to stress the utter powerlessness of Hagar and Ishmael: tossed out of the patriarch's house, set afoot in the wilderness with only a few provisions, they are literally at the mercy of wind and wild. To focus only on their forsakenness, however, is to miss a strong current of the narrative: the wilderness is not only a place that exposes their vulnerability, it offers a refuge from slavery and the space where they encounter God. Delores Williams has enriched our understanding of this pericope by focusing on the wilderness as *promise*. In *Sisters in the Wilderness*, Williams offers a subversive reading of Genesis 16 and 21, a reading that moves beyond the typecasting of victimhood, and uncovers Hagar's fierce determination and struggle for her child's survival. Through a close reading of the biblical text and sustained reflection on the gaps in the text (What happens between the time that God opens Hagar's eyes to the well that quenches her boy's thirst and the time that he grows up?), Williams's book provides a sorely needed perspective to readings that have neglected Hagar and Ishmael. "In the Christian context of Paul, then, Hagar and her descendants represent the outsider position par excellence."[2] In Williams' hands, however, the narrative subverts the tendency to label mother and child as victims. Though the wilderness threatens, it is also the place where Hagar and Ishmael cast off the chains of slavery. Here, away from the master's command, they build, under God's grace, the beginnings of an alternative future. Williams suggests that this future involves not becoming attached to another family, where the cycles of patriarchal abuse and racism would merely perpetuate themselves.[3] The detail is sparse in the biblical story: "God was with the boy, and he grew up; he lived in the wilderness, and he became an expert with the bow . . . and his mother got a wife for him from the land of Egypt" (Gen. 21: 20–21).

The wilderness offers the space for this construction of an alternative future because Hagar and Ishmael hear God's voice in it. In an echo of Genesis 16—where Hagar flees to the wilderness, finds refuge, and the presence of God, who promises her abundant offspring—God addresses Hagar and hearkens the voice of her child.[4] At the very point of abandonment—Hagar hides her son, for she cannot bear to see him die —God reveals Godself to mother and child: not in clouds of glory, but in a voice and in water that saves their lives. The wail of the child in the bushes is the very voice that God hears. Though it is tempting to allegorize the resolution to the story, as if God provides the spiritual drink to all who thirst, such allegory trivializes its life-and-death impact. This is a story about biological survival and the promise of continued flourishing in desperate circumstances. God hears the cries of abandonment and responds, empowering mother and child to keep on living. As Williams notes, this story has immediate resonance in a world in which the faces of the poor, homeless, and hungry are increasingly children and women. The story does not offer the cheap grace of spiritual salvation, but the water necessary for the life of the poor.

The only significant gap in Williams' attention is the relative neglect of the character Ishmael. Though the focus on Hagar is brilliant, and fosters a biblically informed womanist theology, Hagar's son fades quietly into the background. The cries of the child in the wilderness, as a result, are heard not as loudly. This neglect is strange, since it is *Ishmael's* cries that God hears. Genesis 21 is about a mother's desperation and childhood vulnerability, the life-and-death struggle of a banished child, to whom God makes God's very self known. God attends to the cries and pain of *both* mother and child, recognizing that the well-being of one is bound up with the other. Ishmael's cry of abandonment also becomes the occasion of God's grace, and exposes a divine presence that has been with the child *throughout* the wilderness. At the threshold of death, God reminds Hagar of the promises God has made to her and provides the water that saves her child's life.

The agony and refuge of the wilderness offer the beginnings of a new story, in which mother and child will thrive: "The Genesis 21 narrative suggests that Hagar and Ishmael fared well, because God was with the child as he grew. Both the Genesis 16 and 21 narratives reveal the faith, hope and struggle with which an African slave woman worked through issues of survival, surrogacy, motherhood, rape, homelessness and economic and sexual oppression."[5] This is not a story about God's pity for the poor, or God's condescension to those on the fringes; rather, this story centers on a mother and child whose very vulnerability becomes the locus of God's grace. God does not condescend to those in need, but uplifts mother and child in their vulnerability and empowers each to stake out a new future: out of the wilderness, out of this child, a great nation will arise. Their story begins in hunger and thirst but opens to a God who quenches their thirst and assuages their hunger.

At the same time, this interpretation of Genesis runs the risk of the happy ending syndrome. The reality of life for most children at the beginning of the twenty-first century is unlike Ishmael's new beginning in the wilderness. For an increasing number of children worldwide, hunger remains the abiding reality. Every three seconds, a child somewhere on the planet dies of malnutrition: that equates to approximately one thousand children every hour, thirty thousand every day, ten million every year who die because of lack of food.[6] The scale of global hunger has now approached levels that defy the imagination of the biblical writers, expose the effects of human greed, and throw open the age-old question, "Where are you, O God?" The vulnerability of the Ishmael/Hagar story is not a vulnerability unto death: rather, it is a vulnerability that opens up into life: Stripped bare, Hagar's eyes are opened to God anew, and she is empowered by God to live out her days in freedom, away from the chains that enslave. The vulnerability of most of the world's children, however, is markedly different: exposed to hunger, thirst, and disease, they become the stepping-stones for first-world privilege. In the twisted logic of the marketplace, the prosperity of the first world is built upon the backs of those who labor and die in the developing world—backs that often belong to children. If Genesis 21 should expose anything in our North American context, it should be that vulnerability is not an end in itself: it is both the way God makes Godself known, and the occasion for us to twist God's revelation into a bolster for our own privilege while preying upon others. In the former, vulnerability is for the sake of life; in the latter, it becomes a sickness unto death.

WHO ARE THE CHILDREN? THE ILLUSION OF SAMENESS

So far this project in theological anthropology has dodged the central question of *who a child is.* I have been writing as if the reader had an operative understanding or image of the child that informed the argument of the book: a specimen of the species *homo sapiens* between the ages of birth and eighteen. Defining a child, however, is fraught with difficulty. A lauded stage of childhood, at least as Americans often understand it, is a fairly recent development, emerging with the growth of the middle class in the nineteenth century.[7] An extended period of childhood play, sheltered from manual labor, is undoubtedly foreign to many societies in the world, where survival dictates the relatively early stage at which children must work. Ages of entrance to adulthood vary greatly from culture to culture. Attempting to forge a least-common denominator to the varied understandings of childhood and children across cultures is probably as unwise as it is impossible. Nevertheless, the word *child* remains, across a wide variety of cultures. Clearly, most—if not all—societies mark some lines of distinction between children and adults.

The problem becomes even more acute once we recognize that those who typically define and assign differences tend to be those in power. Children, presumably, have little say in defining what a child is. Modernity, with its penchant for rationality, has tended to mark the difference between child and adult in terms of the degree to which one is self-consciously "rational," capable of self-reflection: children are rationally less self-possessed than adults. Yet the marker of rationality unleashes its own set of demons, and ipso facto excludes from personhood (both adult and child) those who fail to measure up to an arbitrary criterion of rationality. One is left asking whether an infant or a comatose teenager is to be considered a child as well, or something else? As Ian McFarland has written, supposedly clear delineations between persons and nonpersons are fraught with difficulty, bias, and even horror: "Because the criteria used to define personhood are in practice shaped by the dominant group within society, acknowledgment as a person invariably brings with it pressure to assimilate to this norm."[8] The abundant difference of graced human life under God is invariably smothered once a standard is fixed to mark what humans, or what children, are. The differently shaped lives of all the world's children are thus harmonized, and no longer enrich and challenge our understandings of ourselves. In McFarland's view, this homogenization will always exclude the marginalized.

McFarland's alternative to defining the "essence" of human persons is to ground an understanding of personhood in a prior understanding of the Triune God who creates humanity in God's image and in Jesus' claim upon all human life. Defining human persons, in other words, is a misguided enterprise, since "knowing what we are as human beings is less important than knowing who makes us what we are."[9] The God who creates us in love is marked by difference in three persons, and we reflect some of the abundance of that difference in the multiply shaped lives that defy any criterion of human essence. In McFarland's analysis, "If the *imago Dei* refers not to some *thing* within us, but to some *one* outside of us, then we are freed from trying to justify our status through the critical examination of others or ourselves. What matters is our relationship with Jesus as the decisive common factor in our lives as human persons."[10] McFarland's account of human personhood is helpful for this project insofar as it uplifts difference as one prerequisite for abundant life in God's world and as it prohibits the penchant of the powerful for defining and excluding the powerless. It suggests that to be a child is to partake in the enormously varied course of human life around the globe. To understand children in God's image, moreover, is to reject the multiple attempts to mold children in *our* image. Children of difference draw life from the God who creates in difference, not from parents and economic systems that impose themselves in molds of suffocating uniformity. To be a child, then, is to begin this course of life —nothing more, nothing less.

Though this definition of childhood as the beginning of the graced and different life given by God does not satisfy criteria that require marked lines between children and adults, only such a loose understanding of childhood will do justice to the abundant difference of God's world and to all persons created in God's image. In what follows, I will attempt to mark three traits of this loose understanding of childhood: less a common essence of childhood than marks of differently shaped children's lives. To be a child is 1) to be chosen by God; 2) to be open and vulnerable to the grace that makes life possible; and 3) to be a pilgrim, oriented God-ward and toward the present. When the church attends to these dimensions of children's lives, it evinces a distinct ethics. A theology of childhood rests not simply in *understanding* children, but radiates outward in circles of *care* and *advocacy* for children. Theological attention opens the church to the children in its midst, whether beyond or within the sanctuary's walls. When the church attends in this manner, children will thrive, rollicking in the unique imagination, play, and prayer that each child brings to the world.

CHILDREN OF ELECTION

Children are chosen by God. This theological statement indicates that children are loved because of the simple fact that *they are*. Doubtless, too many children do not experience love directly; in the throes of starvation and the cyclone of domestic abuse, children know more hate and indifference than love. The posture that we display toward children too often betrays our own disdain for them. God's posture toward children is different. This interpretation of childhood begins with the doctrine of election intentionally, because children are created in God's image, not ours. Election distances a theology of childhood from utilitarian considerations, where children are considered worthy because of something they possess (such as beauty) or provide (such as happiness to a parent). A revised doctrine of election claims first and foremost that children are worthy because God chooses them as subjects of divine love; the primary value of children is not found primarily in some aspect of the creature but in the gracious initiative of the Creator.

Commencing with the doctrine of election, however, is a risky proposition. In careless hands, this doctrine can be twisted easily into an arbitrary divine decree that pronounces some children worthy of salvation while others are not. Much of the history of the Reformed tradition, in fact, swings suspiciously in this direction. As soon as the ink dried on the pages of Calvin's *Institutes*, some systematizers of the tradition seemed bent on specifying the parameters of God's electing grace. Calvin's doctrine, to be sure, has tensions of its own—including its problematic understanding of reprobation—but its central chord is germane to a theology of childhood: it resounds with the graciousness of life itself.

In an era that "tracks" children at earlier and earlier ages—diagnosing gifts that some children possess while others lack—election is decidedly countercultural. For Calvin, God's gracious choice of persons, is "founded upon his freely given mercy, without regard for human worth."[11] Election rests not in the relative value of the creature, but in the freedom of the Creator. This de-centering of the self subverts all attempts to create a hierarchy of value, which inevitably considers some children to be more valuable or gifted than others. Instead, the doctrine of election points to the "undeservedness with which man can receive and respond to the fact that God has chosen and determined and made Himself his God."[12] Calvin, however, invokes double-predestination, an account that we have good reason for rejecting: "God has chosen whom he has willed, and before their birth has laid up for them individually the grace that he willed to grant them."[13] The strength of this position is apparent: an embrace of children that precedes their arrival on the scene. The corresponding shortcoming, however, is painfully obvious: it consigns some children to damnation before birth.

The oddity of Calvin's understanding of election is that it places limits on God's grace. Despite his warning against penetrating the secret depths of divine wisdom, Calvin claims, "by God's bidding . . . salvation is freely offered to some while others are barred from access to it."[14] The flip side of election to blessedness is eternal reprobation. Apparently, for Calvin, God's gracious choice does *not* extend to all children. On my reading, as well as many others since Calvin, this understanding of reprobation effectively limits God's saving grace, and questions his own insistence that God's eternal yes to creation precedes our arrival on the scene. Karl Barth recognized this tension in Calvin's theology, and has offered a Christocentric account of election and rejection. Christ is the one, for Barth, whom God eternally elects *and* rejects; he is the chosen one and the one judged in our place, in whom God's eternal yes is extended to all: "Man is not merely [God's] handiwork and possession. Beyond that—in answer to the call of God—he is His covenant-partner, who has not merely been given existence, but who is appointed for salvation, to whose existence He has given the end of eternal life. . . . Man is the elect creature of God . . . [God] does not renounce the grace of election and the covenant. He does not yield in His will to save."[15] God does not choose to condemn, but to reconcile: "Indeed, God did not send the Son into the world to condemn the world, but in order that the world might be saved through him" (John 3:17).

A doctrine of election that attends to children expands Calvin's conception of grace and betokens universalism: God's electing grace is the embrace of *every* child in God's love. God's election of all children precedes our choosing of any child and our tendency to value some children more than others. God loves and values children simply because *they are.* In a society where genetic technologies promise a day in which parents will be able to select the "best" traits for their own children and filter out what is undesirable or unworthy, election proves subversive: God values infinitely those who are seen as disposable and valueless. God's electing grace is the eternal yes to our tendency to say "no" to children. We neither choose children, nor do they choose us; an eternal choice precedes both parent and child.[16]

Calvin teases out some implications of election with the metaphor of adoption: a word that has immediate bearing and resonance with children. Whereas in many contexts adoptive childhood—overtly or implicitly—is viewed as something different than, or even inferior to biological childhood, for Calvin adoption is honorific, connoting the intimacy of God's relation to humanity. For Calvin, there is no question: the "real" parent is the adoptive parent, whether divine or human.[17] "By free adoption God makes those whom he wills to be his sons; the intrinsic cause of this is in himself, for he is content with his own secret good pleasure."[18] Each child, by adoption, is God's child. In an era in which biological parenthood has reached obsession status in the developed world—witness the bewildering and costly array of fertility treatments—this stress on adoption reminds us that parenthood and childhood have little to do with genetics. Children are not "ours" by virtue of biological makeup, but because of the covenantal and caregiving relationships in which we support children. In this sense, *all* children are adoptive children: chosen by God and entrusted to our care, Ishmael of Egypt, Teleza of Malawi, Hannah Grace of Texas. Here we sense the ethical implications of election: children chosen by God are given to us; that gift demands our response. What scandal it is, what departure from God's covenantal embrace, when we sense responsibility only for those children who live under our roofs, when some children are seen less worthy of care than others.[19] Adopted by God, children are entrusted to our care and vulnerable to the world. In acts of care, moreover, we rediscover the fragility of life itself, and the abundant difference of life in creation.

CHILDHOOD VULNERABILITY IN DIFFERENCE

Chosen by God, children are created in the image of God. Living in God's image, children are metaphors of openness to the One who creates each of us differently. Despite bourgeois longings to the contrary, there is no such thing as a model child, for the shapes of children's lives are as infinitely varied as the stars in the heavens. A second dimension of childhood, therefore, is the vulnerability-in-difference that marks children's lives.

The English word "vulnerable" stems from the Latin root, *vulnerare*, to wound. To be vulnerable is to expose oneself to possible harm and injury—to live on the edge, open to the world's profound beauty and its threatening violence. In societies that prize security and protection —in this respect contemporary America is strikingly similar to the

Greco-Roman world—vulnerability is hardly a virtue to be praised. Yet this is precisely the focus of Matthew's infancy narrative, the way the baby king exposes the false security of power and privilege. As Lynlea Rodger has written,

> Matthew's portrayal of the child is not in the genre of romanticism nor is it naïve. In the infancy narrative Jesus is portrayed as the divinely begotten son (*huios*), but he is also the vulnerable child (*paidion*) who, with his equally vulnerable mother, is threatened from the beginning by powers inimical to the *teleos* appointed for him. It is the weakness and vulnerability of the child Jesus which mark him out as the true king and which subsequently form the center of his teaching which is framed around humility (e.g., 5:3–12, 11:29) and a humble lifestyle (21:5).[20]

Christ's kingship—the kingship of a child—is revealed in an infant and the rejection of power. The vulnerability of the Christ child resurfaces as Jesus grows into his adult ministry, as he relinquishes his own privilege, and empties himself (Phil. 2:6–8) so that others might fully live and that God might be fully revealed in him. Jesus' vulnerability, in other words, is not a headlong rush into martyrdom, or a hunger for self-abnegation; it is vulnerability unto life.

Focusing on the infant Jesus, we may be tempted to romanticize childhood vulnerability, as if it rendered children ipso facto nearer to God's reign. The discussion of the previous chapter, however, reminds us that the image of God is less some quality that children possess than it is the gifted life in difference that God calls us to embrace. Jürgen Moltmann makes the point well: "The point is not that children are closer to the kingdom of God because of especially childlike properties (like innocence or naïveté that adults have lost), but rather that the kingdom of God is closer to them because they are loved, embraced, and blessed by God."[21] If vulnerability is a dimension of the *imago Dei,* it does not emerge as an essence of children's lives, but in the network of difference and personal relationships in which children live. Children are vulnerable to others, and thus point to the God of Christian faith and the creatures God creates in love.

Theologians have rarely recognized the deep theological dimensions of vulnerability-in-relationship so characteristic of infancy. What some of the classic theologians have dismissed as the hallmarks of selfishness—the wails of hunger, the cries to be held—are actually the marks of relationship and dependence of life in God's world.[22] Infants cry not out of selfishness, but to speak of a profound need for another: one who will provide food, touch, and the soothing presence of human attention. A baby is open to any human being who will assuage that gift of otherness. Infants are vulnerable unto others for their lives; without others they will die. The vulnerability of children, then, is a fact of the God-given relatedness into which all persons are born: though most visible in infancy, we never outgrow it.

The danger in uplifting childhood vulnerability is that we thereby close our eyes to the myriad ways in which vulnerability becomes the excuse for others to prey upon children. We will explore this tragic dimension of childhood in the following chapter, but it is important to keep it in mind from the outset. Human relatedness is liable to rupture and destruction. The gifted difference of our lives is such that we can also choose to ignore difference, and thus use others as objects for our own self-aggrandizement. Citing the litany of ways in which children are objectified—through labor in sweatshops, the predations of the sex trade, and the marching "success" of the global economy—only scratches the surface of the pain of children's lives. Clearly, the vulnerability of children is not to be romanticized as something intrinsic that renders children closer to God. If we extend our view of vulnerability, however, and consider it less a quality that children possess, and more a gift of relatedness from God, then our attention is called once again to ministries of care with children. Children's vulnerabilities become a window on our own, making clear the relationships that exist between all children and adults in our midst. Opening our eyes to those relationships also exposes the multiple forms of abuse that children face, and the places where we, in turn, name violence and rescue children from its scars. Interpreting the vulnerability of childhood rests not in description; it invokes an ethic of care for children.

Pamela Couture has made valuable pastoral contributions along these lines. In her recent work, *Seeing Children, Seeing God,* Couture argues that "caring with vulnerable children is a means of grace, a vehicle through which God makes God's self known to us and to them."[23] Couture is clear about her language. In caring "with" the vulnerable children in our midst, she avoids the trap of paternalism: the privileged adult who knows best and thus bestows grace on the impoverished child. In Couture's account, the dynamic of care is reciprocal: the adult who cares is also enriched and nurtured by the child. Her work is a call to comfort the afflicted, to attest to God's universal election of all children, to denounce the myriad forms of oppression that scar children's lives, and to envision a sustainable future for all children. In the midst of this work, Couture claims, we are not alone: in acts of care and in being cared for, we encounter the living face of God. Couture draws deeply from her own Wesleyan heritage in expanding our understanding of care for children beyond paternalism and toward grace, where "*love* sits upon the throne" and "in an exterior circle are all the *works of mercy,* whether to the souls or bodies of men . . . so that all these are real *means of grace.*"[24] Works of mercy, in John Wesley's eyes, are not tokens of privilege and largesse, but expressions of one's poverty and a means of grace. In works of love we are encountered and fulfilled by God. To turn child-ward and God-ward, then, is one and the same turn.

Following the incarnational trajectory of Couture's proposals, we might also suggest something that is rarely acknowledged in white, "malestream" theology, yet conspicuously present in the gospel narratives: to work with the poor is to appease the suffering of Christ. The oft-memorized biblical verses, "For I was hungry and you gave me food, I was thirsty and you gave me something to drink, I was a stranger and you welcomed me, I was naked and you gave me clothing, I was sick and you took care of me, I was in prison and you visited me" (Matt. 25:35–36), are often cited as injunctions to social justice, but rarely as christological statements. Despite a rich history of mediation—encountering Christ in and through others—malestream theologians have tended to avoid the suggestion that the servants of Christ in any way comfort the Servant. Such audacity, supposedly, would compromise the otherness of the Savior. Yet this care of Christ in and through others is precisely what the Matthean narrative suggests. Jacquelyn Grant has noted the correlation between the suffering of Christ and the pain of his servants that is often prominent in slave narratives. An excerpt of one elderly woman's prayer is particularly striking:

> Come to we, dear Massa Jesus. De sun, he hot too much, de road am dat long and boggy (sandy) and we ain't got no buggy for send and fetch Ooner. But Massa, you 'member how you walked dat hard walk up Calvary and ain't weary but tink about we all dat way. We know you ain't weary for to come to we. We pick out de torns, de prickles, de brier, de backslidin' and de quarrel and de sin out of you path so dey shan't hurt Ooner pierce feet no more.[25]

Servants of the Servant minister with and to him in acts of mercy. Nurturing children's lives, we are also nurtured by them. Might our ministry with children also be glimpsed in this regard—as face-to-face, life-sustaining encounters with specific children and an encounter with the Crucified One who sustains life itself? The audacity of Grant's proposal, it seems, is not its departure from the biblical text, but its recovery of a forgotten chord.

The challenge in ministering with children is that they generally do not make the front pages of the daily newspaper. Couture likens this whispered presence of children to God's own hiddenness: "Both God and children are present in the world, whether we want to see them or not. But God and godchildren do not intrude on our lives. They are behind the scenes, waiting for us to discover them."[26] God is not self-evident in (post)modern life; we more readily insulate ourselves from God's holy and gracious presence than allow ourselves to be embraced by it. So, too, is our encounter with children: to spend time with children is also to be changed by them, though it is typically easier to live in the adult world. But if we spend time with children, pay close attention to their words (or gurgles), their gestures, their responses, their faces, we will not remain the same. In this sense, I would quibble only with one aspect of Couture's practical theology: though we may seek out and "discover" children, they also find us. If caring with vulnerable children truly is a means of grace, that grace comes running after us. We do not find it on our own; children find us.

THE PILGRIM CHILD

Chosen by God, graced by difference, children are also pilgrims—persons who are beginning to question and journey in life. As pilgrims, they reconfigure many popular understandings of pilgrimage, suggesting that the journey is as much oriented to the present as it is to the end.

Robert Coles, after an extensive, decades-long series of interviews with children from multiple continents, socioeconomic backgrounds, and religious traditions, offers pilgrimage as one way of understanding the spiritual lives of children. Ginny, a girl from Lawrence, Massachusetts, offers a version of the pilgrimage: "Maybe God puts you here and He gives you these hints of what's ahead, and you should pay attention to them, because that's Him speaking to you."[27] Certainly, no articulation of the pilgrimage is identical to any other. The abundant difference of human life prohibits any homogenization of the journey. Yet, children are the ones who are beginning their travels. Their undeniable attention to the present and their ability to ask the questions that abide with us throughout the journey are helpful in reframing adult understandings of pilgrimage.

Coles quotes an interview with Dorothy Day, as she reflects on her own childhood:

> In many ways I feel I'm the same person now that I was when I was a girl of nine, maybe, or ten, or eleven. . . . Jesus kept on telling us we should try to be like children—be more open to life, curious about it, trusting of it. . . . [I] remember all the *wondering* I did, all the questions I had about life and God and the purpose of things, and even now, when I'm praying, or trying to keep my spiritual side going, and before I know it, I'm a lit-

tle girl. Some of the things I asked then—asked my parents, my friends, and a lot of the time myself—I'm still asking myself now, forty or fifty or sixty years later![28]

For Day, childhood was a time of wonder, of beginning a journey in the world that continued throughout her life. The point of pilgrimage is not to force all children's experiences into a mold that resembles Ginny or Day. Countless children, for example, never reach the age at which questioning is even possible, and countless others, because of brain injury, may not be able to formulate questions in ways that adults recognize. The point, rather, is to recognize the beginning of the childhood journey, and the remarkable attention that children pay to the present. Children subvert our understanding of pilgrimage in their attentiveness: They are pilgrims not because they are on their way somewhere, not because they are growing up to be somebody, but because they already are somewhere and somebody. Children's pilgrimages call us to become who we already are: children of God, attentive to the surprise and mystery of creation.[29]

When nurtured with the basics of food, shelter, intellectual stimulation, emotional support and physical comfort, children present an alternative mode of pilgrimage: a delight in the journey itself, where any goals are incidental. To be a pilgrim as children are is to live in the present, and to pay close attention to the immediacy of the journey. In striking contrast to goal-oriented and consumer adults, young children have little conception of the future: When I promised my three-year-old daughter that her cousins were coming to visit in two weeks, this meant almost nothing to her. She asked when they were coming several times each day in the intervening two weeks. She knew they were coming, was delighted in their coming, and expected them to arrive *now*. This present-orientation of childhood pilgrimage is not hedonistic, but the immediate delight of God's world: an orientation that is not simply on the self, but on self-with-others.

These marks of the pilgrimage offer an example of a kind of Godward existence that we find in many of Jesus' teachings in Matthew. "Can any of you by worrying add a single hour to your span of life? . . .

Consider the lilies of the field, how they grow; they neither toil nor spin, yet I tell you, even Solomon in all his glory was not clothed like one of these. . . . So do not worry about tomorrow, for tomorrow will bring worries of its own. Today's trouble is enough for today" (Matt. 6:27–34). The mistake of some conceptions of pilgrimage, from the mystics to New Age movements, is that God-ward orientation entails a turn from the world. In his classic text, *The Soul's Journey into God,* Bonaventure writes of the final stage of the mystical ascent:"Little or no importance should be given to creation, but all to the creative essence . . . leaving behind all things and freed from all things, you will ascend to the superessential ray of the divine darkness."[30] As valuable as this strand of the tradition is—for its apophaticism and critique of materialism—the danger of some strands of the mystical way is its inattention to the present, the body, and the world. The pilgrimage of children offers an important companion to the mystical way, and shows us that a radical orientation to the present and paying attention to this world are also the marks of God-ward existence.

More significantly, however, children reorient us: back to the relations that ground the Christian worldview in the first place. Their pilgrimage is our summons to attend to the children that surround us. Their present-orientation affirms the enduring value and significance of human relationships. As S. Mark Heim has written, "The Christian view is in many ways a metaphysically pedestrian one. Christianity resolutely affirms and accepts attachment to 'middle' realities of ordinary life: persons, relations, community, communion."[31] As Christian faith anchors hope in relationship (God with us), the flourishing of children's relationships is one component of living out that faith. If we pay attention to the multiple dimensions of children's lives, they will thrive, perhaps exhibiting the playfulness, imagination, and prayer that surface when children flourish.

CHILDREN AT PLAY

These subsequent marks of childhood all children do not share in common. Playing, imagining, and paying attention require as prerequisites

54

ample physical and emotional nurture. Too many children across the planet are too hungry to play, too malnourished to pay much attention to the world around them. Children's laughter, undoubtedly, can be smothered by the specters of hunger and disease. Yet even in the direst of circumstances, fragments of play and laughter can emerge.[32] When we allow children to thrive, the unmistakable sounds of their playfulness will be heard in the streets and across the countryside. Their play infects our own, inviting us to play with them, intimating God's delight in creation.

Few theologians have explored play as a dimension of theological anthropology. It has become almost common wisdom that play is something we outgrow, or at least transform, as we grow older. A necessary diversion, perhaps, from the adult world, play for children has little bearing on the kind of persons God calls us to become. In the mid-nineteenth century, in the crucible of New England Calvinism, Horace Bushnell offered an alternative explanation of children's playfulness in his classic, *Christian Nurture*. Though plagued by patriarchy, some of his remarks on play are helpful even today, and place play at the center of a renewed understanding of the person created in God's image.

To a culture clenched in the fist of revivalism, convicting all (including children) of sin, Bushnell urged his readers "that the child is to grow up a Christian, and never know himself as being otherwise."[33] To a society basking in its own conquest of the Western frontier, celebrating the rugged individualists who obliterated anything and anyone who resisted, Bushnell wrote of interconnection and the well-being of self-with-others. "The Scriptures . . . maintain a marked contrast with the extreme individualism of our modern philosophy. They do not always regard the individual as an isolated unit, but they often look upon men as they exist, in families and in races, under organic laws."[34] This theme of "organicism" permeates nearly every chapter of *Christian Nurture;* to be a human being is to recognize that my life is bound up—for good or for ill—with the life of others. True human being is being-with, and this is especially apparent in the relation between parent and child.

In spelling out the organic nature of human life, Bushnell offers one of the most important reflections on play in the history of Christian theology. Play is one dimension of the organically connected life, in which children instruct *us*. Parents who nurture, in turn, are nurtured in play by their own children. Bushnell describes the beginning of life as a "joyous gambol," which religion too readily suppresses by "needless austerity."[35] The problem with religious instruction, in his eyes, is the same problem with parenting: it dismisses play as irrelevant to the life and thought of mature human being. Rather than seeing play as something confined to the fancies of childhood, Bushnell would extend its joy to all generations and facets of human existence. "Play is the symbol and interpreter of . . . Christian liberty. . . . God has purposely set the beginning of natural life in a mood that foreshadows the last and highest chapter of immortal character. . . . As play is the forerunner of religion, so religion is to be the friend of play."[36] In refreshing counterpoint to the legions of "how to nurture" books that have been written in the decades since Bushnell, his advice to parents is simple: play with your children. "Sometimes, too, the parent, having a hearty interest in the plays of his children, will drop out for the time in the sense of his years, and go into the frolic of their mood with them. They will enjoy no other play-time so much as that . . ."[37] As Bushnell closes his book on Christian education, the reader hears not the stern admonitions of the Sunday school teacher, but the echoes of parents laughing and running with their children across the grass.

In Bushnell's eyes, children's play is sacred *and* subversive. It resists the imposition of oppressive adult responsibility and refuses to accept the dogmatism of inflated adult religiosity. Bushnell describes childhood as "the paradise of nature behind us," which, when we recollect it, or when we play with children, anticipates "the paradise of grace before us."[38] When given the opportunity and nurture, human persons are God's children who play. Children, moreover, show us what the shape of play looks like. Unlike many other forms of human activity, play is strangely resistant to structures of domination and control. To play with someone, by definition, is not to control, but to let be. What is really enjoyable about children's play is not the activity that one has structured, but the *surprise* that comes in the midst of it: not the goal of eluding "it" in the game of tag, but the tumble in the grass as the child tries to escape another's clutches; not the game itself, but the unexpected turns that come *within* the game. "Structured play" is at best an oxymoron. Play itself is subversive to structure, particularly those structures that exclude, dominate, and oppress. Play, as Bushnell notes, "wants no motive but play."[39] Its joy is found not in reaching some kind of goal, but in the delight of the others with whom we play. We can see this if we watch the faces of children at play: this delight in the moment, this sense of connectedness to their playmates. Because we cannot play—at least for a sustained interval—with ourselves, play illumines the difference of humanity as well. Play requires *others* who are different from oneself, whose delights do not necessarily mirror one's own. To play with others is to reconnect to the vulnerabilities and otherness that make each one of us a child of God. Perhaps by playing with children, we recognize again our undeniable need for each other. When we delight in the beauty of a child at play, we rejoice in the mystery that the child *is*.[40]

Playing with children, moreover, is a form of paying attention. One does not play with children to avoid responsibilities for them, but to be opened anew to children and even be guided by them. As Bushnell reflects on play, the child leads while the adult follows. Indeed, the closer one reads Bushnell, it becomes increasingly clear that the nurture of children is at the same time the nurture of the caregiver. When we attend to children and play with them, adults, too, are changed.[41]

For Bushnell, this play evinces a decidedly eschatological bent. The biblical text that frames his discussion of play is from Zechariah's vision of Zion's restoration (Zech. 8:5). "And the streets of the city shall be full of boys and girls playing in its streets." God's redemption of God's people will echo in the laughter of children, as surely as the elderly will once again sit in the streets (v. 4). The new city will include people of all ages, and will value those people for who they are, not for who they might be, or used to be. When the streets of many cities in the world contain children begging rather than playing; when the elderly are confined to institutions in the so-called "developed" world, Zechariah's dream is far from reality. Yet we can catch glimpses of that dream, and the God who delights in all children, whenever we join in the laughter of children at play.

IMAGINING CHILDREN

When given the opportunity, children's play will soar to imaginative heights that confound adult realists. In our house, play with Hannah Grace often involves several characters that I cannot see: an imaginary brother who lives under the bed, imaginary neighbors who come for tea, imaginary fish that swim right under our noses. At play, children can construct imaginary worlds, littered with sprites, wild animals, and spectacular landscapes.[42] One response to such vivid images and characters is to dismiss them as childish flights of fancy that they will soon outgrow, just as we did. Another is to consider them compensatory, somehow making up for a deficiency in a child's life. However appropriate each response may seem, both involve a subtle dismissal of the profound depths of children's imagination, and the fact that children dream and imagine other realities.

When children imagine, they construct alternative spaces by drawing on experiences wholly their own. Imagining other worlds helps them make sense of *this* world. I am always struck by how Hannah Grace orders her imaginary landscape—animals and people have a place that she readily describes. When she invites others into her world, she tells them how to proceed. Her imagination, in this respect, has shaken up my own understanding of how I parent, and it encourages me to see alternative possibilities, indeed infinite possibilities within the family and world, as our relationship grows and responds to each new day. This connection of the imagination with other possibilities, I would argue, is profoundly theological. Christian faith, after all, envisions the transformation of relationships (even broken relationships), imagining them all in the very life of God.

Few theologians of any age have discussed the role of the imagination as perceptively as Samuel Coleridge. In his religious epistemology, the imagination holds an integrative function. By imagining, human persons participate in genuinely poetic and creative moments, drawing together experiences and ideas in cohesion. More than understanding, imagination helps us pay attention and make sense of the world. Yet it also exists, so to speak, on the border between madness and sanity. The imagination, in other words, can easily be dismissed as irrational just as readily as we dismiss children's fancies. At heart, for Coleridge, imagination is part of what drives reason and unleashes its creativity. The one who imagines is also the one who creates, grounded in the God who says "I am who I am; I will be who I will be."[43]

If we follow Coleridge's lead, we are summoned to a renewed appreciation of children's imagination. The God who imagines us empowers us to imagine a world in which God's reign comes to all. The imagination, thus glimpsed, is not an escape from reality, but an intimation of the reign of God that is always expressed in imaginative terms. The Bible is full of unrealistic images that depict the coming of God's reign: where the wolf lies down with the lamb; where the child plays over the adder's den; where swords are beaten into plowshares; to a land flowing with milk and honey; to a New Jerusalem with a river of the water of life.[44] Imagination lies at the heart of Christian faith. When children imagine, they invite us to come along with them, to open our eyes to the present we might not see otherwise. To nurture the imagination is to care for children.

CHILDHOOD ATTENTION

When children thrive, they will play and imagine. In the best of circumstances, children display an abandon for the present, unimpeded by self-imposed goals for the future, unfettered by ghosts of the past. This ability to live in the present allows children to pay close attention to the faces and living things that surround them. Their attention, however, is not indiscriminate: anyone who has spent even a day with a young child will know that children will become restless and distracted if the object of attention does not in some sense involve them. Often, it seems, these moments happen in Protestant mainline worship services, which, apart from hymn-singing and children's sermons, generally do not involve children in worship. Childhood attention is not disinterested, but passionately involved. Children will pay close attention to anything—particularly things like bugs, puddles, and sticks—that adults have been conditioned to ignore.

I have become more aware of the remarkable depths of childhood attention on neighborhood walks with my daughter, Hannah Grace. Journeys to the neighborhood park, a mere three blocks away, can often take an hour if we take them at her pace. Hannah Grace takes her time with things and considers many of the same objects along the way, every day. She pets our cat, lingers over the rose in the corner of our yard, stoops to touch a fence that surrounds a neighbor's flower bed, sticks her nose in the crevice of a pecan tree, traces her finger over letters embedded in the sidewalk, turns her head whenever she hears a bird call. All things can hold her interest; in her eyes all things are new and have a life of their own: the cat, the rose, the fence. Hannah Grace considers these things and invites those who accompany her to do the same.

Her attention, and the attention of many children, often spills over into questions, the questions that children have been asking for millennia: "What do flowers eat? Do squirrels have mommies and daddies? Why did that tree die?" These questions, if we listen to them, can renew our own attention and rekindle awareness of the vulnerable connections that permeate creation. As Bonnie Miller-McLemore writes, "Children see what adults have long since failed to note. They ask questions, thousands of questions, that challenge the way life is lived. They attend religiously to the world's creations; moon, water, sand, fireflies, thunderstorms, are greeted with a certain respect and intrigue."[45]

This passionately involved mode of attention, this willingness to ask the questions that adults are often afraid to ask, is a posture akin to prayer. In one of her characteristically penetrating essays, Simone Weil writes, "Prayer consists of attention. It is the orientation of all the attention of which the soul is capable toward God."[46] If children often pay close attention to the world that adults have shut out, then this attending is a kind of prayer. Prayer, I am convinced, is not foreign to the lives of children—even children for whom organized religion is unfamiliar.[47] Rather, the attentiveness of prayer is quite resonant with the present-orientation of children's lives. Children undoubtedly need to learn the language of prayer, the ritual forms that have sustained communities of faith for centuries. Yet the posture of prayer seems somehow akin to children's own attending and their own questions, if we will only listen to them. Perhaps this is part of the wisdom of the Shema:

> Hear, O Israel: The Lord is our God, the Lord alone. You shall love the Lord your God with all your heart, and with all your soul, and with all your might. Keep these words that I am commanding you today in your heart. Recite them to your children and talk about them when you are at home and when you are away, when you lie down and when you rise. Bind them as a sign on your hand, fix them as an emblem on your forehead, and write them on the doorposts of your house and on your gates. (Deut. 6:4–9)

Here faithfulness to God and attending to one's children are bound inseparably together. Adults recite prayers to children both because they need to learn prayer and because they already are beginning to pray. To learn to pray is not to learn alien speech, but to pay closer attention to the world that surrounds us and to the God who creates that world in love.

Weil's remarks on prayer, however, also display a streak that the experiences of children throw into question. As she spells out the dynamic of prayer, she privileges detachment over attachment, emptying the mind rather than filling it: "Attention consists of suspending our thought, leaving it detached, empty, and ready to be penetrated by the object. . . . Above all our thought should be empty, waiting, not seeking anything, but ready to receive in its naked truth the object that is to penetrate it."[48] Weil, in other words, considers disinterested attention preferable and more prayer-like than passionately involved attention. Detachment and disinterest, however, rarely mark children's lives; their experiences are consummately immediate. I would not claim to know what my daughter is thinking when she attends to the flowers in our front yard; I do not presume whether she understands the prayers that she says before bedtime—this adult presumption intrudes on a conversation that is uniquely her own. Yet, if we walk with children for any length of time, we will notice that their mode of attending is not of the kind that empties all thought, that detaches itself from the subjects of their attention. Rather, it is a mode of attending that connects oneself to the subject, which involves the self in the source of fascination and questioning. Perhaps this kind of attending is also critical to the life of prayer; perhaps it is that component of prayer that allows us to see attention to the world and attention to God as one and the same turn. To pray as children pray is not to lose oneself in God, but to involve oneself in God, or better said, to open one's eyes to the God who is already passionately involved in us. The child who attends is also the child who prays; her prayer invites us to do the same. If adults cannot live wholly in the present in the way that children can—living only in the present would relinquish our responsibilities for working toward a more livable, sustainable future for children—then perhaps, by paying attention, we might learn from them how to pray. Their attention, in other words, summons our own: to them and to God.

CHILDREN OF THE FUTURE

The God who creates the universe in love gives birth to human beings in God's image. In this chapter, I have argued that the *imago Dei* presents itself not as a static imprint that conveys a common human essence, but a relational grace that makes diversely shaped human lives possible in God's world. Children, as partakers of this grace, are chosen and blessed by God, born into the world in positions of vulnerability. Childhood vulnerability offers an intimation of human life with God: open to relationship with others, attentive to the world, passionately involved in the life of the present. When children thrive, there is a delight in life that is unmistakable, a delight simply because life is. Lynlea Rodger has written that children in the gospel narratives are metaphors of hope and openness: "The child as a metaphor is capable of being a carrier as a universal symbol in a world of diverse particularities and typologies characterized by pluralism. The child is both a carrier of the heritage of the past, and represents for the future also an open possibility. It is an archetype which entails mystery, hope, coherence, wonder, and openness to life itself."[49] Given this legacy of the symbol of the child in Western Christian traditions, it is tempting to romanticize childhood and see it simply as a time of naïve innocence.

To lapse into such flights of fancy, however, fails to do justice to particular children in the biblical witness, and to the countless suffering children in today's world. We fail children if we see them only as a faceless symbol of hope; we attend to them only when we are drawn by their unique faces. As the Hagar and Ishmael stories remind us, to be a child is also to be at the mercy of a world that seems to care little about children who are different. If children's vulnerability renders them open to the world, it also means that they are particularly susceptible to violation by predators, both individual and systemic. Violation and violence permeate the world of children, and in countless instances destroy remnants of childhood. Closing our eyes will not help them. Only by paying close attention to the violence that afflicts children's lives can we arrive at a better theological understanding of childhood, and more importantly, offer the kind of prophetic witness and care that will protect and nurture each child chosen by God. To this task we now turn.

FOUR

Vulnerability and Violence

 majority of the world's children live under a constant threat of violence. Their lives hang by a thin thread of connection to the abundant life that God bestows and invites us to embrace. Imperiled by grinding poverty, beset by infectious diseases that could be eradicated, subject to sweatshop labor, threatened by a growing sex trade and proliferation of child pornography, and by wars that devour, children experience contempt in all quarters of the world. Every culture, it seems, lauds childhood as a special time, yet these same cultures—particularly our own—are often inattentive to the children in their midst. To be a child in today's world is also to be subject to violence that takes many forms and innumerable lives. Our world daily witnesses thousands of children's gratuitous deaths. When death—whether by the stealth of abject poverty or the pierce of a bullet—forms so much of the tapestry of childhood, it is no small wonder that children endure. And yet somehow, in some way, many children do endure, embracing life in the midst of death-dealing.

The turn in this chapter is to the realities of children's lives that most adults in the West are apt to ignore: the near-ubiquitous suffering of the children among us, both across the street and across the world. My intention in this space is to move beyond a romanticized understanding of childhood and face the haunting circumstances that surround so many children's lives. Focusing on these present threats to childhood will better enable us to understand—and critique—the language of sin as it applies to children. As I will argue, much of the classic conception of sin falls short in addressing the reality of children's lives. One wonders whether the language of sin itself is adequate in interpreting the lives of children and in summoning our energies, under God's grace, to better children's lives. By offering a subtle shift in perspective—from the agent of sin to the victim of sin, and by suggesting that children are victims *and* agents—we might better speak the gospel of salvation in a world of suffering children and better live in attentiveness to the children among us. This turn to the threatened state of childhood will take three steps: first to the state of the world's children; second to the in/adequacies of the language of sin in relation to that state; and third, to a critical reconstruction of that doctrine in response to the children in our midst.

THE STATE OF THE WORLD'S CHILDREN

Theology worthy of its name pays attention to context. No matter how faithful any work is to the Bible, no matter how adeptly it addresses the multiple voices within church history, no matter how lucid its exposition of philosophical themes, theology falls short if it does not squarely face the present. Karl Barth's dictum of keeping the Bible in one hand and the newspaper in the other is germane: any theology that professes to stand in the tradition of the Word made flesh must grapple with the flesh that the Word assumed. If we don't pay attention to our particular strands of humanity, in their dazzling divergence and surprising convergence, we pretend that we do not inhabit any context, and we make theology an idle projection that does not interpret the good news *for us.*

A theology of childhood becomes a charade if it does not pay close attention to the concrete realities of children's lives across the globe. To interpret childhood, one has to ask oneself, "where are the children, and what do their lives look like? How are they nurtured, how are they threatened?" Asking these questions, however, defies pat answers. Children are everywhere—and their lives are both nurtured and threatened at all times and in all places. I simply cannot account for the circumstances of *all* the world's children—in places as disparate as Zimbabwe, Bolivia, and Denmark—especially within the span of a work such as this. Painting a generalized picture of the world's children fails to pay attention to particular faces and needs within those contexts. Yet, some attention to the common threats that imperil children's lives is warranted. Though children are endangered in different ways and degrees throughout these contexts, the children of the world may share at least one thing in common: their lives are often threatened by the systemic violence of poverty, disease, war, and malnutrition. To understand childhood vulnerability, we must also glimpse the ways in which vulnerability renders children susceptible to injury and death.

Poverty and Vulnerability

Current estimates of the world's population hover around 6.1 billion, with no signs of decrease in the foreseeable future. Of those more than 6 billion, more than 1.5 billion are children under the age of eleven (approximately one-quarter of the world's population). Numbers this size are scarcely comprehensible, yet they confirm that the family of humanity is steadily increasing, and with that increase comes a surge in the numbers of children, particularly in the so-called "developing" regions of the globe. What are the economic realities of those children? According to a recent United Nations report, more than one-half billion of those children (one-third of the world's children) live on less than one dollar per day.[1] This means that for every two children who live at, or above a mere subsistence level, one struggles under the weight of a grinding poverty that inscribes the world in stark terms. Begging and the uncertainty of one's next meal are the bread of daily life for ever-growing numbers of the world's children.

In our heralded era of globalization, which—if we listen to its vocal proponents—will bring prosperity of the world's resources to people all over the planet, the effects of this promise have yet to be felt, and quickly become nightmares. The wealth of the planet, which is indeed vast, is increasingly becoming concentrated in the coffers of a few nations. Initial results of globalization appear less a trickle-down enrichment of all God's children and more the triumph of planetary plutocracy. The same UNICEF report notes, "The gulf between the richest and the poorest countries on earth is actually widening with every passing day. In 1990 the annual income per person in industrialized countries was 60 times greater than that in the least developed countries; in 1999 it was almost 100 times greater."[2] Concentrations of wealth of this magnitude are nothing less than an affront to the promise of God's reign; embedded within a society that has benefited enormously from globalization—though certainly this benefit has not been extended to all—Christians in North America are called upon to name their own participation in the violence of the global economy, and pray and act under God's grace in envisioning a different world.

From the relative comfort of technological societies, it is easy to distance oneself from the jarring realities of poverty. Many in the West consider poverty a problem of the Southern Hemisphere—somewhere across the globe, but not in our hometowns. A glance beneath the veneer of prosperity, however, yields alarming results. Enormous concentrations of wealth are growing within the so-called "developed" nations as well. "Over the past 20 years . . . there has been a growth in child poverty in almost every country in the European Union and the proportion of public expenditures on children has diminished—at a time when there has been a consistent period of economic growth during which overall wealth has increased."[3] Clearly some have benefited economically because of mushrooming stock portfolios, but in general, these beneficiaries have *not* been children. From children's perspectives, the era of globalization is bankrupt: the success of some is achieved at the expense of poor children's lives.

Lest one suppose that the growing gap between rich and poor is a problem felt only across the Atlantic, a turn homeward presents equally disturbing results. Thirty-seven percent of children in the United States live in low-income families, defined in 2002 as $27,772 for a family of three. When the focus turns to children under the age of six, the numbers increase to 40 percent.[4] A stubborn fact of life exists embedded within the ardent hope of the American dream: the younger a child is in the United States, the more likely s/he is to be poor. As Marian Wright Edelman has written: "Every 44 seconds, an American baby is born into poverty."[5] The effects of such poverty are disastrous, and rarely are met with public commitments that serve the interests of children. In fact, trends point to even worse circumstances for the poorest children in the United States: since 1979 "the top 5 percent (3.6 million) of American families saw their average income increase by $101,000 or 66 percent, while the bottom 20 percent (14.4 million families) lost $184 a year from their average income of $13,500 in 1999 dollars."[6] American children are more likely to be poor now than at any time in the past thirty years. Such statistics are particularly disturbing if we take into account the phenomenal growth of the U.S. economy between 1999 and 2000: an increase of one-half trillion dollars that was "thirteen times the sum needed to lift the incomes of all below-poverty families with children to the poverty line."[7] Even if we consider the contraction of growth in the United States since 2000, the machinations of the economic engine clearly do not, by and large, consider the state of our children. At best they are considered potential consumers, but certainly not beneficiaries of an elusive economic dream. The scandal is that an alternative is certainly possible: if some would be willing to live with less, many of our children could live more abundantly. Current realities, however, leave the vast majority of the world's children on the outside of that dream, looking with hungry eyes inward.

Health and Vulnerability

The reality of poverty cannot be reduced to economic statistics. We cannot understand its effects in raw monetary terms, because the torrent of poverty breaks into other dimensions of human life. When children are born in poverty, their lives also tend to be marked by inadequate health care, diminished access to education, and lack of basic nutrition. The essential provisions of human life prove more elusive. When we turn our attention to the state of the world's children, the picture is anything but encouraging. In 2000, for example, 27 percent of children under age five in developing countries experienced severe or moderate malnutrition.[8] This is not the kind of nutritional deficit characterized by lack of vitamins from time to time; this is oppression that places children on the brink of starvation, significantly deprived of nutrients so that normal physical and mental development is arrested. The basic stages of childhood, under such grinding conditions, are subject to severe disruption. Thankfully, malnutrition rates have begun to decrease in most quarters of the world—with the conspicuous exception of sub-Saharan Africa.[9] Yet such gains have been incremental, and it is unclear whether the slowdown in the global economy will reverse the gains that have been made thus far.

Another face of the global health crisis is met in children with HIV/AIDS and those who have lost either or both parents to the disease. The stealth of the AIDS pandemic has orphaned more than thirteen million children under age fifteen in the world.[10] HIV/AIDS is killing parents and children in countless corners of the developing and developed world. In many of those corners, even the most rudimentary forms of public health and sex education are inadequate, resulting in the seemingly dim outlook for those children's futures. Because of HIV/AIDS, children face the ever more real prospect that they will face the rest of their lives without parents.

Child Labor

A whirring global economic engine allows people of privilege in the West to buy electronic goods, current clothing fashions, and athletic shoes at relatively cheap prices. But who labors in the factories that produce the baubles of consumerism? In many instances they are children, who provide perhaps the ideal workforce for multinational corporations: they require less, they have less power to organize themselves, and because of their size can often slip into dangerous spaces where adults cannot. School-age translates into working-age for many of the world's children, with girls being particularly likely *never* to attend school. Worldwide 60 percent of children who are not in school are girls; many of those girls wind up in the labor force as domestic workers, where girls between the ages of twelve and seventeen make up a full 90 percent of the world's domestic workers.[11] Working in the homes of more affluent families, unprotected by even basic labor laws, domestic workers are often subjected to physical intimidation and sexual abuse. Powerless, with no supervision other than the immediate employer, these girls often live under the same roof with the abuser.

Perhaps the most sordid stories of child labor involve the children who are forced into the sex trade. Teenage girls are the most likely population to be victimized by prostitution, but are certainly not the only ones affected by its scourge.[12] The words of Taiwo, a thirteen-year-old Nigerian, are haunting in their cadence:

> Imagine in a family where there is a boy and a girl, the girl will do all the work in the house. If there is any sacrifice to be made it will be the girl that will suffer it, for instance, when the family income is down the girl will be sent to go and hawk, that is to sell things in the streets and along the highway. Most times they will push her out to an old man or introduce her into prostitution. Even our mothers are also guilty of this act. This is very wrong, people of the world should change their attitude towards girls and women.[13]

A bourgeoning business of sex tourism in Southeast Asia and proliferation of child pornography on the internet and elsewhere would not be possible were it not for the wealth of many (predominantly in the North) who prey on the children of the South. A more glaring example of the contempt of children is scarcely imaginable, than the all-too-frequent scenario in which children are seen as nothing other than objects of sexual abuse, and in which poor families feel they have no other alternative than to sell their children into such trades. In Taiwo's story, the dangerous chords of sexism, classism, and contempt of children form a hangman's noose, destroying the lives of the child sold into slavery and the family who lost a beloved member, all in the name of a few dollars to buy the next few meals and the twisted sexual gratification of a rich stranger.

Children live in poverty throughout the world, and this reality of life renders them susceptible to a host of other threats: insufficient education, the specter of AIDS, the looming ghost of the sex trade. Statistics fail to measure the full effects of poverty; these effects can only be measured by the loss and diminishment of each child's life. Whereas adults may be resilient to lingering effects of poverty upon their lives, often children are not. As Pamela Couture writes, "Five or six years of poverty in an adult life may be painful but endurable. Five or six years of poverty in the life of a child influences a third of that child's formation."[14] Those years mark a stealth violence that shapes a child's vision of the future, the world the child comes to know. Violence also comes in more explicit forms—from domestic abuse to war—and scars innumerable children, rich *and* poor.

Domestic Violence and Crime

Households and homes have figured prominently in Christian vocabulary since the New Testament era. Early Christians worshiped in each other's houses; many of Paul's letters refer to the responsibilities that members of the household have to one another; the Protestant Reformers rediscovered the centrality of the home and family in the Christian life; Horace Bushnell called families "little churches;"[15] and many feminist theologians have pointed to the ways that classic understanding of home and family have proven destructive to women's lives. Though the configuration of members and roles within the household has undergone dramatic change since the first Christian century, the image of home has enormous staying power. For many, this image connotes security and refuge, housing persons who are committed to one another in covenants of love, where children are welcomed, nurtured, and challenged. Yet for many children, home is less a haven than it is hostile ground.

Adrienne Rich has suggested that home is the most dangerous place in America for women.[16] Behind the shuttered windows of domesticity rages a fury of domestic violence: Men who beat—and even kill—the women in their lives. Covenants of love degenerate into abusive patterns of relation, while children who witness these patterns are damaged beyond measure. When boys witness men abusing their partners, whether verbally or physically, they are more likely to perpetuate such patterns in the future. Likewise, when girls glimpse mothers who do not flee domestic violence, they may be more likely to tolerate abuse in their own relationships. Physical and emotional violence suppurates like a boil within the household, and its presence is becoming rampant, perhaps especially in bastions of privilege. A 2000–2001 UNICEF poll of children in Europe and Central Asia notes, "6 out of 10 children reported violent or aggressive behavior at home."[17] In the United States, current estimates of the numbers of children who witness domestic violence in their homes hover between 3.3 and 10 million.[18] Obviously, home is often a dangerous place for children and mothers.

An alarming number of children not only observe violence, but are themselves victims of violence in the home. In 1998, according to the Department of Health and Human Services, some 2.9 million children in the United States were "reported as suspected victims of child abuse and neglect."[19] Since incidences of domestic abuse are chronically underreported—children often do not have access to channels of law enforcement and justice—the numbers are greater than any statistics suggest. Child abuse, in our society that purportedly celebrates childhood, is a decidedly hidden scourge: whispered in the corridors of state agencies, but rarely broached with the frankness that it deserves. While adults remain silent, children continue to suffer.

As the highly publicized scandal in the Roman Catholic Church has reminded the nation, the specter of child sexual abuse has gone unacknowledged for far too long, especially in the church. Nothing less than a conspiracy of secrecy has flourished in the ecclesial hierarchy that strives to protect the perpetrators of crimes while barring the healing of the childhood victims. Under the guise of priestly confidentiality, the lives of countless children have been damaged irreparably. Protestants who would suppose that this scandal is merely a "Catholic problem" are guilty of ignoring—and even fostering—the abuse that exists within their own ranks. Pedophiles are the property of no one denomination. When the church continues to remain silent, or merely handles the problem in the hushed tones of embarrassment, it smothers the voices of the children and perpetuates a climate that tolerates violence. Church then becomes not a sanctuary for children, but a hostile den of abuse.

When sexual violence is tolerated in the church, few channels exist for the prophetic denunciation of violence against children in society. Current scandals imply that the church simply mirrors, rather than critiques, our society's dangerous fusion of violence and sexuality—a fusion that invariably preys upon children. In the United States, children comprise 71 percent of all sex crime victims; children under the age of twelve, moreover, are particularly vulnerable to predation, constituting a full one-third of all victims of sexual assault.[20] Perhaps the most damning aspect of a culture that mixes violence and sexuality is that it seizes the youngest in our midst as sexual objects.

The violence that children face in American society is symbolized by sexual predation and an obsession with guns that defies the standards of other Western nations. The debate over gun control continues along its customary course in the United States, with ardent proponents of gun rights lined up against advocates for more restrictive measures governing their possession and use. Stakes are high and the money spent by the advocates of gun rights is enormous. Meanwhile, children continue to be killed in our streets, homes, and schools, at the rate of approximately ten children per day.[21] The violence of our streets claims not only the lives of young children, but devours adolescents as participants in the cycle. Losses in inner-city communities are particularly devastating. As Pamela Couture notes, in the late 1980s, "about one-fourth of teenage males ages fifteen to nineteen were lost to inner city communities through death and incarceration."[22] Whether confronted with the barrel of a gun or the violation of rape, children bear a disproportionate share of the violence that infects the body of the nation.

As children are scarred by knives in the streets, they become susceptible to further participation in an endless cycle of violence. Children
and adolescents, to be sure, are capable of murder and rape (often because that is the world they have learned from others). In response,
American society has proven remarkably willing to mete out the death
penalty. The 1989 U.S. Supreme Court decision declaring that the ex-
ecution of juvenile offenders does *not* constitute cruel and unusual
punishment was quickly followed by several executions of persons who
committed crimes before the age of eighteen. In doing so, the United
States has joined the ranks of six other nations with dismal human
rights records: The Democratic Republic of Congo, Yemen, Iran,
Nigeria, Pakistan, and Saudi Arabia. While a few of these nations have
executed one juvenile offender, the United States has killed the most
(nineteen). Nationwide, eighty-two juvenile offenders now sit on death
row in fifteen states.[23] When a society willingly executes persons for
committing crimes before the accepted age of adulthood, it has given
up on young people. Childhood, for these imprisoned young people, is
not only dead; their lives, in the eyes of their nation, are suitable for
elimination.

Children and War

Another stubborn fact of the global age is the incessant raging of war.
The past century has not proven more humane than others, but has
demonstrated the alacrity of the human race in resorting to battle. In
Jan Oberg's words, "The twentieth century is probably the most war-
ridden of all in Western history; at least 100 million human beings lost
their lives in war—on average 3,500 a day."[24] In our age, children absorb
war's effects: they lose their lives, limbs, and even fire the weapons that
dismember other children. "Between 1990 and 2000, 2 million children
were slaughtered, 6 million injured or permanently disabled and 12
million left homeless" because of war.[25] The wars of the late twentieth
century are not global conflagrations on the scale of the World Wars;
rather, they are smaller in scope, but more relentless in their swath of
destruction. Feeding on xenophobia, nationalism, and religious funda-

mentalism, the wars of the early twenty-first century tend to be waged in the poorer regions of the globe while the rich nations profit from them. When we Americans insulate ourselves from war—pretending that we do not participate in the battles that rage elsewhere—we absolve ourselves from the profits made by our death-dealing. The United States is now the world's largest supplier of armaments, from handguns to bombs of mass-destruction. As Walter Lowe has written, our sickness is that we "know these weapons of destruction only as something *positive*! They strengthen our country, they fuel our economy."[26] In a twisted farce, the economic well-being of the nation is bound up with the deaths of those who do not benefit from the New World Order.

Lowe suggests that Americans now live in a permanent war economy; we export arms and heavily arm ourselves. The cash flow that sustains our defense industries is scarcely comprehensible: "one and a half billion human beings live every day on one-third the amount every American spends on weapons every day."[27] Engines of economic growth in the United States are sustained, in large part, by weapons that ensure the death of thousands in our city streets and millions around the globe. When we turn our eyes from this reality, we deny our own participation in death-dealing that lurks under the guise of prosperity and close our eyes to sin. Is there any more significant betrayal of Jesus' promise, "I came that they may have life, and have it abundantly" (John 10:10b) than closing our eyes to violence, particularly when it claims the smallest among us? Childhood vulnerability, in our threatened world, is not an innocence to be romanticized, but a decidedly mixed blessing—rendering children susceptible to violence and losing life just as life begins.

Neglecting Children

Innumerable scourges threaten children's lives throughout the world—poverty, disease, child labor, domestic violence, and war are but a few of them. The state of the world's children is a state of neglect, despite attempts and proclamations in nearly every culture to uphold children.[28] In middle-class American life, the neglect of children often takes more subtle forms. Herbert Anderson and Susan B. W. Johnson, in their work *Regarding Children,* claim that in our generation of unprecedented economic prosperity, we foster "a *culture of indifference* toward our children."[29] Children, they argue, "change things"—marriages, careers, even worldviews—yet this change is the very reality that our upwardly mobile society resists and resents. Our culture pretends that we can have it all without losing a thing, and supposes that one can care for a child without making any sacrifice, or adapting one's life to a child's pace. Children, however, stand that assumption in question by calling for our attention and disrupt, however playfully, any tendency to become engrossed in something at the expense of children.

Johnson and Anderson relate an anecdote that has countless parallels throughout the suburbs, and suggests that the American Dream rarely accounts for children. One girl whose "parents have professional careers with complicated schedules," usually waits for her harried parents long after practice has ended. One day, with tears in her eyes, she tells her coach, "I'm terribly inconvenient."[30] Her remark is as stark as it is revealing; when career takes precedence over all else, children bear the brunt of professional sacrifice. The myth of quality time so abundant in bourgeois American society is that parents and caregivers can somehow make up for lost time and missed opportunities with children, either in the late evening or on weekends. But children have no concept of quality time; time is all that they have, and once it passes, opportunities disappear. The American Dream, which promises success and prosperity to those who prostrate themselves to professional gods, holds children mostly as an intrusion in the dream. This girl's story calls us to regard children as other than an intrusion—and as a welcome disruption of hollow dreams. Her story calls for nothing short of a reorientation of human life that proceeds more according to the pace of children, where children are not "American dreamers in the making," but the attendants of grace, who redirect our attention to the world. At present, however, children's lives are often characterized by multiple streams of neglect, all of which carve destructive channels. When the state of the world's children reveals this neglect, how does the Christian vocabulary of sin address children's lives? Where does our language suffice and where does it fall short? To those questions we now turn.

A BRIEF TOUR OF THE DOCTRINE OF SIN

The doctrine of sin in the Christian church never reached the degree of controversy that preceded the early councils (and continued after them) on questions of Christology and the Trinity. Though Christians have argued among themselves on the nature of sin, its character as original guilt, and how it is transmitted throughout the human species, the Christian church bears no definitive, early statement on sin and salvation. Perhaps the dispute between Augustine and Pelagius best approximates the discussions on Christological orthodoxy; however, unlike the rough consensus (undoubtedly enforced by the fist of empire) that emerged in the wake of Chalcedon, the dispute between Augustine and Pelagius continues even today. If Augustine is granted the status as the most influential early exponent of the basic tenets concerning sin, he is by no means its definitive interpreter. What emerges from any cursory glance at the history of Christian thought, instead, is an abundance of imagery and reflection concerning sin. The doctrine, in other words, rests not in an orthodox definition, but in diverse attempts to bespeak the tragedy, brokenness, and rupture of human existence in God's world. At its best, the doctrine makes this attempt by describing sin not chiefly in terms of individual, sinful human actions, but in the ambiguous and tragic condition that nurtures and destroys human life. Though many theologians from across the ages would agree that sin is expressed best as a *condition* (and not an action), most connect human activity in some way to the state of human sinfulness — either as sin's cause or its result. The consequence, unfortunately, has been that the language of sin, most generally speaking, has reflected primarily the experiences of those in power. Too infrequently has the doctrine been glimpsed from the underside, of those whose condition is the result of others' abuse of power: the poor, the oppressed, the children. This brief tour of the language of sin in the Christian tradition, therefore, is not meant to be a full account, but an expression of the adequacy and inadequacy of various approaches to sin, with particular attention to children.[31]

Pauline Foundations

The New Testament abounds with language about sin, and in the midst of its abundance stands Paul, whose letters express both the soaring grace of God's creative will and the abysmal depths of the human condition. In these epistles to specific Christian communities, Paul's understanding of sin betrays not the precision of the systematician, but the craft of a poet. His intent in addressing sin—particularly in the Roman and Galatian correspondence—is not to expound a doctrine, but express the righteousness of God revealed in Christ, and to expose the condition of all human beings who fall short of that righteousness. His letter to the Romans makes extensive use of an Adam-Christ typology, which has proved enormously influential in the subsequent history of theology, both as an expression of original sin and an account of sin's transmission from generation to generation.

Paul locates the emergence of sin in a specific, historical event—Adam's transgression of God's command—just as he locates justification in history, Jesus Christ. In evocative prose, Paul describes the ripple effect that one person's transgression has throughout creation: "Just as sin came into the world through one man, and death came through sin, and so death spread to all because all have sinned. . . . Just as one man's trespass led to condemnation for all, so one man's act of righteousness leads to justification and life for all" (Rom. 5:12, 18). With masterful flourish, Paul links together the transgression of Adam, the righteousness of Jesus Christ, and the world's participation in condemnation and redemption. Adam and Christ thus cast the character of all subsequent history. Adam's sin becomes our own, just as Christ's righteousness makes us his own: "Just as by the one man's disobedience the many were made sinners, so by the one man's obedience the many will be made righteous" (v. 19). Sin characterizes, in Paul's eyes, not isolated actions, but the condition in which *all* human activity takes place. Sin is a permanent state that is only remedied in the righteousness of Christ. In Paul's hand, sin takes on "an almost mythical coloration,"[32] and becomes a looming character in the cosmic drama of creation, transgression, and redemption.

Though sin describes chiefly a state of human affairs, from which we cannot escape, Paul also depicts its effects in relation to individual action. The cosmic character of sin provides both the backdrop for social activity and describes the incapacity of each person to do the good on his/her own. In a passage that has received perhaps more attention than any other in his correspondence, Paul writes: "For I do not do the good I want, but the evil I do not want is what I do. Now if I do what I do not want, it is no longer I that do it, but sin that dwells within me" (7:19–20). The condition of sin, in other words, determines the nature of one's actions. This inner conflict is only resolved by Christ, whose righteousness brings forth nothing less than a change in the believer, "so that Christ lives in and through" us.[33] Without resorting to a lengthy account of how sin emerged in history or reducing sin to a particular action (such as pride), Paul personifies sin and renders it not simply the result of one human's action, but the sea in which all activity swims. In a contemporary context that often seems most characterized by contempt for children's lives, Paul's account may have renewed relevance, not in the sense of blaming children for their own neglect, but by calling our attention to a neglect that all too often precedes a child's arrival.

Augustine's Elaboration

If Paul's account of sin is best described as rhetorical and typological, Augustine's subsequent tackling of the issue takes up the strands of systematic exposition. The figure of Adam becomes for Augustine the example of what happens to each human person, and describes an original guilt that each of us, regardless of age, display in our inmost fibers. Sin precedes us at the same time that we embody it and are responsible for it. Originating in a turn away from God, sin, for Augustine, is perhaps best described as a "self-imposed bondage, a free will that binds itself."[34] Whereas Paul, at least in the Roman correspondence, focuses primarily on disobedience, Augustine singles out human pride in his account of the fall. Though not all sin is pride, Augustine claims that pride is the commencement of every sin, "because it was this which overthrew the devil, from whom arose the origin of sin."[35] Pride is the root of our turning away from God, expressed historically in the Fall, which repeats itself in each new generation and person. Augustine's account is sometimes distorted, as if the turn away from God were a deliberate choice of evil in the face of the known good, God. Pride, for Augustine, has less the traces of a willful defiance than it is the forsaking of the higher good for a lesser good. As Eugene TeSelle has written, "However malicious it may appear to be . . . willing is always for the sake of *some* value, though that value may be insignificant or inappropriate."[36] Sin, whose root is pride, is not a condition of utter inversion (willing evil instead of good), but of subtle distortion. Yet this subtle distortion of substituting one good for the true Good has disastrous effects: all are born in sin, because guilt is transmitted across generations. In Augustine's words: "The fault of our nature remains in our offspring so deeply impressed as to make it guilty."[37] In the end, children are guilty of sin before they even arrive on the scene.

Augustine is aware of tensions in his doctrine that are often overlooked. By locating the root of sin as pride, he suggests that sin bears the traces of the willful assertion of power, or false power (as in the mistaken ability to choose the good). Such an account certainly makes sense in cases where persons in power wield it over others, yet what about the disempowered, what about children? Is the commencement of sin in children also related to an arrogation of power? Such a suggestion obscures the state of neglect that characterizes so many children's lives. Secondly, Augustine at times connects the state of original sin—the brokenness that precedes us—to actual sins that break forth in our own lives. Robert Williams has written that this close connection has its problems: "First, if sin is a hereditary taint, this appears to undermine human responsibility for sin. . . . Second, the claim that all deserve punishment is somewhat plausible in the case of adults, in whom original sin breaks forth freely in actual sins, but would not seem to apply to infants."[38] It is difficult, in other words, to be a strict Augustinian, when our attention turns to children. Augustine was also aware of this:

If even infants, as the true faith holds, are born sinners, *not on their account,* but in virtue of their origin . . . then it follows that just as they are sinners, they are recognized as breakers of the Law which was given in paradise. . . . Yet even so it must be observed that it would be unjust that the soul of an infant should perish, when the child itself was not responsible for the neglect of circumcision.[39]

The judicial metaphor of Augustine's account of fall, guilt, and accountability may not address many of the realities of children's lives and responsibilities. It speaks persuasively to the empowered but turns our attention from the scars of sin in the victims of history. Though it makes sense to describe the sea in which infants swim as saturated with sinfulness, it fails the test of nurture to hold infants accountable for their environment. Though following the threads of Augustine's argument might lead in this direction, this is a step that Augustine does not take. Blaming the victim, from Augustine's perspective, will not be tolerated. Augustine's account of sin, therefore, is not lacking for what it includes, but for what it excludes (the voices of children and victims), and calls for further elaboration, perhaps in ways that Augustine actually anticipated.

Calvin's Reclamation of the Augustinian Legacy

The most prominent heirs of Augustinian understandings of sin appear not in medieval Catholicism but in the work of the magisterial reformers. John Calvin, in particular, lays claim to the Augustinian legacy with his account of human depravity and guilt, but also exaggerates that legacy by claiming that infants are equally culpable for sin. Though Calvin agrees with Augustine in describing pride as "the beginning of all evils," sin does not commence with pride; rather, disobedience is the "beginning of the Fall," while unfaithfulness is its root.[40] Sin, in other words, cannot be reduced to a particular human foible, but is connected to a host of ways in which human persons substitute something else for faith in the one God revealed in Christ Jesus.

If sin displays manifest roots, its consequences are likewise disastrous. Adam's transgression results in nothing less than the destruction of the *imago Dei*. Here Calvin expands the Augustinian legacy by suggesting that nothing of God's image remains in us: "Therefore, after the heavenly image was obliterated in [Adam], he was not the only one to suffer this punishment—that, in the place of wisdom, virtue, holiness, truth, and justice, with which adornments he had been clad, there came forth the most filthy plagues, blindness, impotence, impurity, vanity, and injustice —but he also entangled and immersed his offspring in the same miseries."[41] Whereas Augustine holds out the possibility of a remnant of the *imago Dei* residing in humanity after the Fall, Calvin rejects even this shred of hope. Original sin is marked not simply by the false orientation of humankind (its orientation toward lesser goods), but depravity in its core: "So depraved is his nature that he can be moved or impelled only to do evil."[42] Each human person inherits sin, yet also sins willingly and without compulsion, "by the most eager inclination of his heart."[43]

Calvin's account of guilt and the transmission of sin extends to infants. Small children constitute no special case in the destructive scope of sin: "Even infants themselves, while they carry their condemnation along with them from the mother's womb, are guilty not of another's fault but of their own."[44] The strength of Calvin's position is that infants constitute no tertium quid. They are not adults-in-the-making as so many other strands of theology have suggested; rather, they are already fully human, and as such are fully responsible for sin. But this same insistence on the depravity of infants, however, assumes that the adult model of the moral agent is the normative lens for understanding sin. Calvin's understanding of individual sins assumes a degree of willfulness—the human person as actor—and pays less attention to the complexities of human behavior in which we are both actors and acted upon. Perhaps this complexity is best glimpsed in the youngest of children: infants respond to action and initiate their own action, they act and are acted upon. To suggest that we can identify sin in willfulness alone or receptivity alone is a simplistic reduction of human behavior, particularly regarding infants. To his credit, Calvin never wrote at length about the topic of sin in infants: he did not consider it an important subject in its own right, which if stressed wantonly could lead to the neglect of children.[45] In fact, Calvin's most suggestive writings about infants in the *Institutes* occur not during the discussion of sin, but in his understanding of baptism and covenant.[46] Nevertheless, Calvin's stress on the sinner as actor (and not as acted upon) constitutes one limitation of his writing, and calls for some revision in attending to the lives of children.

Schleiermacher's Relational Theology of Sin

Friedrich Schleiermacher anchors his conception of sin in a thoroughly relational understanding of the human person. We are creatures who live in a continual state of utter dependence on God. Echoing Calvin's refrain that we are not our own, but God's, Schleiermacher broadens that refrain to include dependence on *others*. If living an authentic human life is perfect consciousness of our interconnection with others and utter dependence on God, sin is living a lie, as if one were not connected to others and not dependent on God. Sin is turning away from who we are, a rejection of our God-given lives of being-with, and alienation from God. Schleiermacher's favored expression is to describe sin as a profound lack of God- (and self-) awareness. "The only course open to us is to reckon everything as sin that has arrested the free development of the God-consciousness."[47] The less we are aware of ourselves as utterly dependent, the less we develop into the creatures that God intends us to be. We are responsible for this lack of awareness; we cloud our minds and pretend we are something else. Schleiermacher's doctrine thus affirms Augustine and Calvin in reckoning us responsible for sin.

Three significant implications emerge from this re-articulation and recovery of the doctrine. First, Schleiermacher does not ascribe to the gradual perfectibility of humankind, as if the closer we come to God, the more our sin disappears. Rather, the deeper the development of God-consciousness, the more profound one's awareness of sin becomes. Sin is a tragic dimension of the human condition that becomes painfully manifest the more we rest in dependence on God. Secondly, Schleiermacher rejects Calvin's position that the sin of Adam resulted in a drastic change in human nature: from original righteousness to total depravity. "We must accordingly adhere to the position that the idea of a change in human nature entailed by the first sin of the first pair has no place among the propositions which rank as utterances of our Christian consciousness."[48] To emphasize a complete change in human nature, Schleiermacher argues, is to lessen the significance of each person's guilt—each person's free turning away from others and God—entailed in the rejection of our God-given humanity.

Perhaps the most revolutionary move in Schleiermacher's anthropology, however, is his suggestion that original blessedness also entails a tragic dimension, that the arresting of God-consciousness is somehow bound up with human being. Schleiermacher does not regard the metaphor of Eden as synonymous with perfection, but as righteousness *and* tragedy:

> If . . . we discard the view that a change took place in human nature itself, but . . . still maintain that an incapacity for the good is the universal state of men, it follows that this incapacity was present in human nature *before the first sin,* and that accordingly what is now innate sinfulness was something native also to the first pair. . . . Yet it must be so construed as to be compatible with the equally inherent original perfection of man, and in such a way that the state of the first human pair is understood to have been throughout analogous to our own.[49]

In his seemingly heterodox suggestion that Adam and Eve bear the traces of an original imperfection as well as original righteousness, Schleiermacher retrieves a theme that had almost disappeared with the ascendancy of Augustinian theodicy. Here, the champion of modern theology recovers a theme best evidenced in the work of Irenaeus, who suggested not a schema of creation (perfection) and fall, but an eschatologically oriented cosmic drama, where the imperfection and tragedy of earthly life is recapitulated and redeemed by Christ. In Irenaeus' prospective narrative, the perfection of the human creature is located not in Eden, but at the end of the story.[50]

Schleiermacher's articulation of sin, which combines surprising Calvinist and Irenaean sentiments, yields ambiguous results when we turn our attention to children. By suggesting that tragedy and imperfection are mysteriously built into the cosmic tapestry from the beginning, Schleiermacher decenters the autonomous moral agent. Sin is still characterized by a willful rejection of our God-given humanity (turning away from relationship), but this willfulness does not exhaust the story. Sin also describes the brokenness of community and relation that precedes our arrival on the scene. Schleiermacher thus questions Calvin's understanding that infants are guilty of sin, but affirms that they are "born into" sin. His resolution of this problem centers on his understanding of the development of the God-consciousness. As we grow in consciousness, we become more deeply aware of our sin and hence more culpable for it. Infants, who presumably do not exhibit the same degree of self-consciousness as adults, are thus less culpable for sin, however much it surrounds them. Schleiermacher's conception helps move an understanding away from any kind of framework that blames the victim of sin or minimizes its effects on the most vulnerable in society. In a world that is often characterized by the abuse and contempt of children, Schleiermacher's exposition helps describe the brokenness of human community that often preys on the youngest.

At the same time, Schleiermacher's anchoring of sin within a selective understanding of God-consciousness risks marginalizing the youngest in our midst. By focusing on self-awareness, and God-awareness, Schleiermacher seems from the outset to relegate the consciousness of infants and very small children to the fringes. Just as those who are not fully conscious are not as culpable for sin, those same persons seem less reflective of relatedness to God and others. His strongly relational theology, in the end, focuses chiefly on an understanding of consciousness that may not be characteristic of *all* human beings. Surely, the mystery of human relation and of relationship with God confounds the boundaries of self-consciousness. One is not any less a child of God simply because one does not display the traces of mature, adult self-awareness. Perhaps the case is precisely the reverse—especially if we follow Schleiermacher's own argument—that those most dependent on others, infants and the infirm, display in vivid form what it means to be a child of God.

Rita Nakashima Brock: Sin as Symptom

One of the most provocative works in feminist theology of the last several decades is Rita Nakashima Brock's *Journeys By Heart*. In arresting prose, Brock re-crafts Christology and sin by introducing the abused child as the unwitting victim of much classical theory. Traditional theologies of atonement, she argues, have reinforced the image of a Father-God who exacts satisfaction from his rebellious children, and thus endorse patriarchal understandings of the human family that feed on submission and abuse. In the face of theologies that valorize submission unto death, Brock offers a Christology of "erotic power" that resonates with some strands of Schleiermacher, but most significantly with process thought and feminist protest. In a striking rereading of Mark's gospel, Brock allows the voice of the victim to speak: personified in an abused female child. This girl symbolizes the person who has been violated by patriarchal structures of abuse; this child is the often-unacknowledged victim of theologies of sin that would blame her and leave no room for her cry.

One of the first moves of Brock's work is to reject Augustinian theodicy: "I am suggesting that sinfulness is neither a state that comes inevitably with birth nor something that permeates all human existence, but a symptom of the unavoidably relational nature of human existence through which we come to be damaged and damage others."[51] Sin stems not from a human propensity toward disobedience, pride, or lack of faith, but is more a reflection of the ambiguity of human relationships. The same connections between us that give birth to new life are the connections that abuse and destroy. "Sin is a sign of our brokenheartedness, of how damaged we are, not of how evil, willfully disobedient, and culpable we are. Sin is not something to be punished, but something to be healed."[52]

Brock's account neither offers a theory of how sin emerges (she rejects Augustine), nor does it offer a denouement that resolves the effects of sin in a tidy package (she also questions Irenaeus). Rather, her work allows us to pay attention to the brokenness that surrounds and envelops human life, and to empower us to stand with the erotic power of life in the midst of death-dealing. Even the story of Jesus offers no joyous ending: "The death of Jesus reveals the brokenheartedness of patriarchy. His dying is a testimony to the powers of oppression. It is neither salvific nor essential. It is tragic."[53] Jesus' crucifixion does not redeem sin so much as it exposes it in vivid detail. It does not bolster divinely sanctioned child abuse, but points to the fracture of creation itself. The narrative of Jesus, in this sense, is subversive, privileging the children who suffer in our midst. This story, in the end, focuses not on Jesus' death, but on his life and resurrection—which embraces the victims of a patriarchal world.[54]

Brock's work is one of the few in the tradition that pays specific attention to children in its conception of sin and salvation. It offers no norm of adult rationality or moral agency. Rather, it pays close attention to the victims of sin, who are often children, and simply calls our attention to their faces. Hers is a theology that allows us to acknowledge the tragic that in the end is inexplicable—even in light of Christ's redemption of humanity. The glimmering of an understanding of sin "from the underside," from the perspective of the child, thus comes into closer view.

TENSIONS IN THE DOCTRINE OF SIN: WHERE ARE THE CHILDREN?

Christian understandings of sin are as varied as the ways in which the reality of sin slithers in human life. Even among the few theologians just surveyed, wide discrepancies exist: where Augustine offers a historical account of the origin of sin, Brock rejects the idea that sin inevitably precedes our birth; where Calvin describes the obliteration of the *imago*, Schleiermacher questions whether human nature is changed after the Fall. Amid such difference, harmonization is impossible; yet some broad consistencies emerge. Each theologian suggests that sin describes a pervasive, suprapersonal reality rather than individual actions. Sin is the sea in which all human activity swims. In describing this transper-

sonal reality, however, most theologians have in one way or another re-
lied on accounts of moral agency that assume a certain degree of
power. The universal guilt of sin—whether addressed by Augustine,
Schleiermacher, or Calvin—has tended toward descriptions of willful
activity: the power to turn away from the ultimate Good or to deny
one's fundamental relatedness and thus inflict damage on creation, others, and ultimately one's relationship with God. With few exceptions
(Brock's work constitutes one of them), most articulations of sin have
paid enormous attention to the perpetrator and left little room for considering the victim. Here we run up against one of the greatest challenges in articulating a theology of childhood: How to describe the
horror that children face, how to call our attention to the suffering inflicted by sin, without lumping children into a rather ill-fitting mold of
willful agents who have, at least in part, brought about their own misery.
As Pamela Couture has written, "A theology of children and poverty
faces the complicated task of describing, without minimizing, the
agony that many children bear and the behavioral problems that become symptoms of that agony. The traditional language of sin, evil, and
depravity does not allow us adequately to articulate the problem."[55]
Perhaps the classical doctrine of sin is strongest in calling our attention
to the fact that brokenness and suffering precede any child's birth: all
children, in this manner, are born into sin. Yet, the doctrine stumbles
when it attempts to give an account of the original guilt of all persons.
To put it bluntly, are children and infants really as guilty of the reality
that precedes them as adults? To claim as much, I would argue, is to obscure the suffering that results from sin and absolve our responsibility
for the children in our midst.

In light of these difficulties, we may be tempted to consider the antitype in the tradition: children as tabula rasae of innocence, upon
whom are inflicted the lashes of a sinful world. We encountered this
understanding briefly in chapter 1, in the work of Jean-Jacques
Rousseau. This account of original innocence has always proven an at-
tractive option in Christian theologies that sought to avoid consigning
children to perdition. Yet, it has dangers of its own, which result in a di-

minished understanding of children's lives. Bonnie Miller-McLemore argues that romanticized understandings of childhood innocence actually strip children of agency: "By picturing children as innocent, adults failed to take them seriously and often abused adult responsibility for earnest protection of children's physical, moral, and spiritual well-being."[56] Children are not passive vessels that absorb the world's impact; they respond and act in ways uniquely their own.

A purely social understanding of original sin, which locates sin in the damage society inflicts on innocent children, can have the unwarranted consequence of depriving children of agency and effectively dooming them to the evils of a hell-bent world. A purely individual understanding of sin, which locates sin in the child born into the world, runs the danger of being inattentive to the enormously complicated set of influences and contexts in which children live their lives. Neither blaming the child nor blaming society alone will do. If the classical tendency has veered toward the former, the antitype has embraced the latter. Neither, however, is an accurate rendition of the damage inflicted by sin.

Janet Pais has stated the problem rather starkly. Her work, *Suffer the Children,* is an attempt to articulate a liberation theology from the perspective of an abused child. One of the most potent critiques she raises about the classical doctrine is that it invariably smothers children's individuality, placing them on a rather large heap of indistinguishable sins. Her challenge is fierce: "Any attitude about good and evil in the child is a form of contempt, because it fails to respect the individuality of the child. Whether we see 'the child' as good, as evil, or as a combination of good and evil, we fail to accept and relate to a particular, individual child as he or she truly is, whatever that may mean. . . . We cannot know the nature of 'the child' in the abstract."[57] The danger, as Pais sees it, is that the doctrine of sin tends toward overgeneralization. If we describe all children as "sinful" or even "good," we are guilty of theological reductionism and are less open to the intricacy and uniqueness of each child's life. Doctrine, in this sense, eclipses a genuine encounter with children.

The tendency of the doctrine runs counter to Jesus of Nazareth's own regard of children. Never do the gospels record Jesus issuing a general pronouncement on children's lives; rather, they relate his personal encounters with individual children: in acts of healing, compassion, and blessing. The examples are abundant, but one in particular stands out: While the disciples argued about greatness in the gospel of Mark, Jesus "took a little child and put it among them; and taking it in his arms, he said to them, 'Whoever welcomes one such child in my name welcomes me, and whoever welcomes me welcomes not me but the one who sent me'" (9:36–37). Jesus takes a child in his arms and makes no proclamation about the child's inherent goodness or internal depravity. He simply tells his disciples to welcome children, in a gesture of personal hospitality. To welcome a child—not in the abstract, but in the particular—is to welcome Jesus and the One who sent him. Jesus calls his followers to pay attention to particular children, and to all children. Theology can only come afterward, in response to that call.

If our understanding of sin remains one-dimensional, focusing primarily upon perpetrators, then we not only neglect the ways in which Jesus encounters children, we may wind up abetting the structures of sin that Christian doctrine attempts to denounce. Andrew Sung Park and Susan Nelson have recognized this insidious tendency within Christian thought perceptively: "The wounds and alienation of the sinned-against require us to deepen our theological reflection. The category of sin by itself is insufficient to tackle the wounds and alienation of the sinned-against. . . . In this sense, we realize that the doctrine of sin can itself perpetuate evil from the victims' perspective."[58] Once we render all persons, all children as the inheritors of original sin, we may erase the distinctions in degrees of culpability and damage inflicted on creation. Where classical theology has tended to place the understanding of evil within the doctrine of sin (evil arises *because* of the Fall), Park and Nelson urge us to "locate the doctrine of sin within the context of the experience of evil."[59] If we make this move, we may better pay attention to the suffering children in our midst in a way that does not connect their experience of evil to a particular historical emergence of sin.

Another antinomy in the classic doctrine, perhaps, is that the human-God relationship is the ultimate trump card in describing sin's effects. Because all relationships reflect one's relation with God, all sin expresses a rupture between humanity and God. This chord resounds in theologians as divergent as Augustine and Brock and rightly connects the relationships within creation to the Sovereign God and Giver of life. One problem with this perspective, however, is that it may verticalize the doctrine of sin in a way that eclipses the significance of creature-creature relationships. Theodore Jennings has suggested that "the emphasis on the violation of God more often serves to divert attention away from the concrete violation of the neighbor. . . . In this way the verticalization of the doctrine of sin comes to serve the interest of the maintenance of the current arrangements of power. For the violation of the vulnerable is ontologically less serious than one's relation to God."[60] Though the relationship with God may be the most inclusive way of describing sin—there is no relation with God apart from God's creation —the intent of the doctrine should serve the purpose of highlighting *all* relationships and the brokenness that pervades them. The relationship with God, in other words, should not dismiss all other relationships as ancillary, but disclose those relationships as bound up with the life of God. The violation of the child, in other words, is not less important than a violation of God, but all the more serious because God takes the suffering of children as God's own. The lives of all children, in this sense, are lived within God, but are not eclipsed by God.

The limitations of the classic doctrine, in short, encompass the general tendency to consider children only as adults in the making. When the adult moral agent is presented as a model for the person trapped in sin, when the doctrine assumes particular arrangements of power, when considerations of "good" and "evil" come prior to consideration of the uniqueness of each child of God, children invariably suffer. The question then emerges whether a complementary understanding of sin can be developed: an understanding that begins with the suffering of children and with a welcome to the children in our midst. The challenge is to *encounter* children before we describe their nature.

FROM THE SINNED-AGAINST?

Children are born into a world that all too rarely cares for them adequately. From the perspective of an abused, neglected, and hungry child, sin does not give birth to evil; rather, evil is the context in which sin arises. From this perspective, sin manifests itself not in pride or the assertion of the self (the child is simply struggling to survive), or in unfaithfulness (the child is trusting that s/he will survive), but out of the experience of being rejected and being considered less than human. In Miller-McLemore's words, "Children are more often sinned against than sinners themselves."[61] When we take stock of the state of the world's children, we understand sin both as postures of refusal (rejecting others) and the "historical experience of *being refused*."[62]

Refusal, being treated as something other than a child of God, bears invariably tragic results. When children are told they are stupid, they begin to believe as much; when they are abused, they internalize those wounds long after lashes have healed and may even consider themselves to blame for their abuse.[63] When the powerful inflict wounds on the powerless, shame in the victim often results. Susan Nelson writes, "To know shame is to experience ourselves as deficient and ultimately rejectable. . . . In this process, what was an experience of shame becomes core to our experience of who we are. If sin is to refuse our human condition and to seek to secure ourselves . . . then shame is born of being refused and is reflected in the sense of being 'defective,' in the corresponding dread that there is no future for 'me.' "[64] When children are conscripted as soldiers for war, they are told they have no future. When American arms exports exceed fifty billion dollars per year, while a child in the United States is more likely to be poor today than twenty years ago, children are told that they do not matter. When a child is raped, the spirit of life is trampled. When time with children is sandwiched between the ridiculous demands and expectations of a workaholic parent's schedule, those children are told that they matter less than arbitrary standards of career. When children are forced into sweatshops, their value is reduced to the cheap goods they produce. Refusal can take many shapes, yet children bear its brunt. Each refusal—whether met with the butt of a rifle, the neglect of a parent, or the fist of violence—bears the message that we are something less than children of God. When this message repeats itself again and again, when children know more refusal than acceptance, more violence than nurture, more neglect than healing, the language of sin and total depravity somehow falls short. This condition of being refused simply cannot be explained as something inherent to the nature of the child. To claim as much is to abet the pernicious tendency of blaming the victim in our culture of privilege.

When we listen to children's voices and pay attention to their experiences in a violent world, we become aware of ways in which the doctrine of sin might be expanded. Nelson is one theologian taking steps in this direction:

> If it is possible that some postures of refusal are born of deprivation (being refused) rather than depravity (an inborn tendency to refuse), this raises some interesting questions for the classic doctrine of original sin. . . . We might understand how human sin (postures of refusal) can be passed on not by an inherited depravity, but through our human vulnerability to being refused, through actual ruptures of the interpersonal bridge that are left unattended, and through the repetition of refusals that are an expression of that unhealed wound.[65]

Sin describes something far more pervasive, far more destructive, and far more complicated than the traditional language of depravity and inheritance addresses. We sell children short when we fall into the tendency of one of two extremes: either attributing all sin to a depravity that pervades each individual or considering children blank slates who absorb willy-nilly the brunt of the world's refusal. The realities of children's lives are far more complex than either of these alternatives suggest: they absorb refusal, but they also rebound; they are remarkably open to the world, but this openness can be slammed shut in an instant; they are both agents in an ambiguous world and recipients of others' actions.

CHILDREN'S VULNERABILITY, ADULT NEGLECT: EXPANDING OUR UNDERSTANDING OF SIN

The point of Christian language about sin is not to explain away the suffering of the world, but to address it in all its complexity and to point to the hope that sin does not utter the final cosmic word. Only by taking sin seriously, in all its facets and from the faces of its victims, does the word of redemption ring as something other than a comforting sop. A renewed understanding of sin, with special reference to children, begins with two convictions: 1) each person is connected in some way to every other—in an age of American individualism, the doctrine of sin evinces the *social* and *cosmic* character of human life; 2) each person is at all times both actor and acted upon—no matter how old or how young, we are never reducible to passive vessels or masters of our own destiny. The tendency to portray children as acted upon and adults as actors does little to address the complexity of sin. We are always both, and the interaction of both renders the disease of sin even more insidious.

Though it is often portrayed as such in neopietist circles, the doctrine of sin is not an isolating doctrine, leaving each individual wallowing in an ocean of depravity, craving a gracious God. At its heart, rather, the doctrine is profoundly relational—connecting each person in some way to every other. Part of the intent in developing accounts of the inheritance of original sin, moreover, was to demonstrate the interconnected nature of the human race. Whether voiced in Irenaeus' cosmic schema of rupture and imperfection, which is recapitulated and redeemed in Christ, or in Aquinas' account of the transmission of sin from one generation to another, sin connects the character of each human person to every other. In twentieth-century America, this profound sense of interconnection was captured in the civil rights movement. Martin Luther King Jr. was effective not only in naming the cancer of racism as sin, but also in connecting its effects to those whites who felt themselves insulated from it: "I am cognizant of the interrelatedness of all communities and states. . . . Injustice anywhere is a threat to justice everywhere. We are caught in an inescapable network of mutuality, tied in a single garment of destiny."[66] The reality of human life is not isolation, but cosmic connection; to live otherwise is to pretend and to lie. Given this interconnection, the birth of a child is nothing less than new life and hope for the world. Yet the reality of most children's births is also anxiety, pain, and suffering: where that child's next meal will come from, whether violence and war will soon claim that child's life. If the birth of a child is a metaphor of hope, then the interconnectedness of life also demonstrates that the suffering of any child invariably ripples throughout creation. Douglas Sturm has written, "The deprivation of any child is, in the final analysis, a cosmic loss."[67] To speak of such connection reclaims the core of Christian relational sensibilities, echoed in such phrases as the body of Christ, the people of God, Holy Communion, and the earthiness of the creation story.[68] Sin speaks to these profound connections, while exposing their fragility and susceptibility to violence.

Given the profoundly relational character of graced human life, how then might we talk about the transmission of sin, how the groans of one child become the groaning of creation? Part of the classic doctrine has been to interpret this transmission in terms of an original depravity that accompanies our birth. Though such accounts offer profuse examples of the inevitability of human sin, they do not always resonate with the experiences of the world's victims—so many of whom are children. Susan Nelson's work reminds us of this lack, and suggests that we stress not the inheritance of sin, but the inheritance of a "vulnerability to refusal."[69] This shift is subtle, but significant. Instead of describing the origin of sin as inherited depravity that is present before we take our first breath, she points to an inherited vulnerability to refusal that results in greater brokenness with each incident of violation. Human beings are thus from the very beginning both actors and acted upon. Infants both experience refusal and embrace and respond with behaviors uniquely their own. This subtle shift pays greater attention to the complexity of human behavior and nature: that we are always and at all times actors *and* recipients of action. The tragic nature of sin, in this framework, is that the very fact of our nature that renders us capable of relationship—our vulnerability—is also what makes us susceptible to violence and rejection. Relation to God and others, in the end, can also be twisted into rejection and despair—pointing to the ways in which we become participants in our own rejection and our need for grace beyond ourselves.

Children, no matter how young, are something more than passive victims in a world of violence. From the beginning, they are participants in a dance of embrace and rejection. Nelson writes: "The dance of the generations is passed on from parent to child as each generation . . . fails to give its children the love they need, thereby breaking their hearts as well. . . . They are locked together in a dance of alienation born of refusal and a broken heart. Tragically, children are more than victims in this dance for they often, out of good hearts, participate in their own rejection."[70] Caressed children are valued and told that the world is full of love; when the caress is twisted into sexual abuse, children are told they are valueless. The messages children hear, the experiences they have, inform and confirm the people they are. When rejection exceeds acceptance, moreover, they may wind up believing themselves only worthy of refusal, participating in their own dance of destruction. Sin's insidious nature is precisely its relationality. Experiencing rejection by others, we also become capable of injuring ourselves and others.

Demonstrated in even the most innocent childhood responses that attempt to compensate for parental inadequacies (the child who apologizes to her parent after that parent has lost all patience and yelled), children internalize the wounds that others inflict. And they often respond to these wounds in ways that further harm themselves. Witnessed in contexts as diverse as alcoholic parents, workaholic parents, or parents who are never satisfied with a child's efforts, children learn to compensate for their parents, and even shield parents from themselves. In the subtle dynamic of a relational world, the wounds of one generation find new and tragic expression in the reality of the next.[71]

Sin, however, is not the first fact of human existence. Rather, sin is the pain and wounding—experienced in the multifarious ways human beings act and are acted upon—of an already graced creation. The vulnerability of our lives is such that we come into the world remarkably open to relationship. An infant cannot survive without others. God chooses us not for who we will become, but for who we are: each infant, each child of God. Vulnerability and openness, as I have argued, are dimensions of the *imago Dei*. If sin is the woundedness of a relational creation—both the wounds we inflict on others and the wounds that we receive—then sin is the aberration of creation. Sin expresses the fundamental disease of human life, which is present mysteriously from the beginning of life, but is neither the fundamental character of life nor its final word. To claim otherwise is to grant sin the trump card over grace, and to ignore the original blessing of each of God's children. This claim of the original graciousness of children's lives has resonance with the deepest incarnational sensibilities of the Christian tradition—expressed in as varied trajectories as John's gospel, Irenaeus, Aquinas, Karl Rahner, and F. D. Maurice—but also with the common experience of a child's birth.

When I held Molly's hand in a Nashville hospital room during early morning hours of February 28, 1999, the birth of Hannah Grace confirmed the grace of life itself. Amid the anguish of a painful labor (which only Molly could describe), and an almost sleepless night, Hannah Grace came into the world. From that mysterious and exhilarating moment where the girl that I loved emerged from the woman I loved, from the moment that Hannah Grace lay on Molly's breast and locked eyes with her, from the moment that she turned her eyes to me, from the moment where Gracie's warm, soft skin, still wet from the waters of birth and the blood of life, rested on Molly's chest and then touched my own, our eyes were opened anew to the gift and surprise of God's grace. Sin was not the first word that gave birth to Hannah Grace. The beginning of her life was not epitomized by depravity and doom; rather, it was graced by vulnerability, relationship, and hope. Yet, at the same time that Hannah Grace came into the world with such promise, she became open to the wounded nature of creation itself. Sin, in this sense, cannot be traced to a total depravity that accompanies birth, but illumines the wounds of the world that invariably cause further wounding. The risk of life is that as soon as we come into the world, the hope and promise of life is threatened by an aberration of life—sin. Whether captured by the violence that surrounds the lives of countless children, the hunger that characterizes much life on the planet, or the lie of adult invulnerability, children act and respond to the wounds that surround and inflict them. Life's beginning bears the traces of the unsurpassable promise of God's grace and the abundant scars of a relational world.

LIFE ABUNDANT: A BRIEF UNDERSTANDING OF SALVATION

One of the appropriate marks of a doctrine of sin that bears resonance to the reality of children's lives is whether it evokes responses of hope. A destructive doctrine of sin, which focuses chiefly on depravity, in the wrong hands can wind up blaming victims for their lot. When we pay attention more to adults than the children in our midst, one has to ask whether our doctrines of sin do more to dispel hope in children than they do to instill it. Theodore Jennings has written, "Perhaps the test that matters most in this process is whether our doctrinal discourse, like the interaction between Jesus and the paralytic, provokes an outburst of praise to God on the part of the vulnerable, humiliated, and violated masses who bear the brunt of the world's sin."[72] Jennings' words are a powerful reminder that the sin we proclaim has to bear some correspondence to the hope given by God's grace in Christ. Sin is not a threat by which we browbeat our children, but the naming of an aberration in the promise of graced life with God. Its blame cannot be pinpointed and reduced to individual culpability, but must be diagnosed as a kind of cosmic sickness, which infects all who live on planet Earth.

A critical recovery of the doctrine of sin may also draw wisdom from those strands of Christian theology generally found in the East, which understand sin primarily as disease and not as inherited depravity. John Wesley is a Western theologian who has hearkened this Eastern tradition. In his sermon "Original Sin," Wesley notes that the religion of Jesus Christ "is *therapeia psucheis,* God's method of healing a soul which is *thus diseased.* Hereby the great Physician of souls applies medicine to heal *this sickness;* to restore human nature, totally corrupted in all its faculties."[73] Salvation, thus understood, is less the removal of a stain that covers humanity than it is the restoration of fellowship between creation and the Creator. Its promise is not simply the purging of guilt from the perpetrator, but the abundant living of the creature with the Creator. Salvation, as healing, is not a promise for the future, but a reality glimpsed, however dimly, in the multiple ways that Christ frees us to live with, for, and by each other and God: right here, right now. Salvation is not a promise we possess, but a gift to live as God's children again. In a world in which the threats to this promise are ubiquitous, what are the ways in which God claims us as children? To that question we now turn, and to specific practices of vulnerability reflected in the ecclesia. The church lives into the promise of childhood when it becomes a sanctuary for children.

FIVE   Practices of Vulnerability

hen violence rends the tapestry of children's lives, the
most natural human response is to shield children from
it. Protective instincts surface immediately when children are threatened. In the face of the life-draining
scourges of poverty, disease, and physical abuse, a necessary first response is to shelter and rescue children. Yet the tendency
among many North Americans is to conceive shelter as retreat. In response to the horrors that imperil children, many Americans protect at
all costs: by moving to gated communities supposedly immune from
crime, by seeking out the best schools that guarantee a cadre of families
similar to our own, thus removing ourselves as much as possible from
the realities that continue to plague children and families who are not
like us. Protection by these means becomes a retreat from the world and
an abandonment of the children who do not live under our roofs.

This same tendency can slither into the lives of Christian congregations. Commonplace wisdom considers church as refuge, a place to

101

gather with others, pray in comfort, be nurtured, and shelter ourselves from a hostile world. None of these longings alone is pernicious, but when longings for safety blend with impulses toward homogenization, the mixture turns deadly. Heaped together, they form the bricks and mortar of a church that withdraws from the world and sees itself only as the protector of those who live within its hallowed walls.

The New Testament's word for church, *ekklesia*, suggests something different: an assembly of people "called out" from the world in order to serve it in the name of Jesus Christ. Retreat is antithetical to that vision; protection alone does not constitute service in Christ's name. In a world torn by violence, the church cannot withdraw in order to protect its own children. Rather, it is called to welcome all children and embody an alternative vision for the world, witnessed in practices of vulnerability central to its sacramental and prophetic life: baptism, peacemaking, sanctuary, and prayer. In these seemingly mundane acts, the church both witnesses to God's love for children made manifest in Jesus Christ, and offers a glimmering of God's embrace of all children. In word and sacrament, the church enacts an ethic of care for children. Becoming vulnerable with children in its prophetic and sacramental life, the church not only protects children, but heralds a reign where their voices are heard. The turn in this chapter is to the more practical dimensions of a theology of childhood. How do the preceding reflections relate to the ongoing life of the Christian church? What are the distinctive practices of a church that attends to children and grounds hope in the Christ child?

The marks of church that I explore here are decidedly eclectic. In exploring how infant baptism invokes the full membership of children in the covenant, I draw deeply from my own Reformed heritage, particularly the work of John Calvin. Sketching the marks of church as a peaceable community, I also rely on the legacy of the Radical Reformation. In the Anabaptist vision, peacemaking is not an appendage to the core claims of church, but bound up with the church's profession of following a vulnerable and nonviolent Savior. I will subsequently explore some historical strands of the church's practice of sanctuary, finally drawing together disparate threads of Christian spirituality in the section on prayer. The result, I hope, is a self-consciously ecumenical ecclesiology that engages children.

This skeletal ecclesiology presents the church as a prophetic and sacramental community that bears witness to a vulnerable Savior in its life and practice. The church, in the end, is less described as a separate, alternative society, than it is a herald for the world of a different kind of reign: where the powerless have voice, where violence rules no more, where children are full members of the covenant. In a North American consumer society that celebrates acquisition, competition, and independence, these movements of the church that care for children are nothing short of strange.

INFANT BAPTISM AND A COVENANT WITH CHILDREN

Debates over the nature and practice of baptism have probably raged since the dawn of the Christian church. They became particularly acute, however, in the Age of Reform. While the magisterial reformers favored the continued practice of infant baptism as witness to the nascent faith of infants and their membership in the covenant, Anabaptists argued that infant baptism minimized the decisive nature of faith and the believer's participation in the sacrament. Such disputes have continued well into the present, with the lines between the diverging camps becoming more blurred. Several Reformed theologians of the present and last century—Karl Barth and Jürgen Moltmann among them—have argued that in an era of cultural Christianity the church is most faithful when it adopts the practice of believer's baptism. In what follows, I offer an interpretation of infant baptism that takes many of its cues from John Calvin. Baptism, in this sense, is an ecclesial practice of vulnerability because it signals a community that belongs to God, open to God's reign when we become humble like a child. When the church baptizes infants, it marks its own vulnerability as children of God, recognizes that the children who are victimized and threatened by the world's violence are already full inheritors of the covenant, and cares for the youngest in its midst. Children do not grow into the covenant; they already partake in it. Infant baptism, thus interpreted, is one ecclesial practice that signals the claim children have on us, though it is certainly not the only form of baptism that commits children to our care.[1]

John Calvin describes a sacrament as "an outward sign by which the Lord seals on our consciences the promises of his good will toward us in order to sustain the weakness of our faith," or "a testimony of divine grace toward us, confirmed by an outward sign, with mutual attestation of our piety toward him."[2] Just as the Holy Scriptures constitute God's "lisp" to us, God's accommodation of the divine Word to human words, the sacraments represent the Word's assumption of flesh. God takes the basic elements of water, bread, and wine and through them "instruct[s] us according to our dull capacity, and to lead us by the hand as tutors lead children."[3] The Word of God makes use of the ordinary: flesh, food, water, and uses them to instruct us and confirm our faith. The sacraments are not keys that unlock the door to salvation (without which we are doomed), but the modes of instruction and edification that a vulnerable God uses to communicate with us. Intriguingly, Calvin uses the metaphor of the child to indicate how the sacraments instruct and nourish us: just as a tutor leads the child in education, so do the sacraments nurture us in the Christian life. From the beginning, Calvin's sacramental theology invokes children.

As he turns to baptism, Calvin's argument takes a striking hue. Arguing against the reigning Roman Catholic and Lutheran practice of "emergency baptism," the practice of baptizing infants who were near death outside a worship service, sometimes by laypersons, Calvin contends that baptism is *not* necessary for salvation. Rather, "baptism is the sign of the initiation by which we are received into the society of the church, in order that, engrafted in Christ, we may be reckoned among God's children."[4] The sacrament does not issue individual passports to God's realm, but instead is a sign by which God's promises of the cleansing of sin and the believer's participation in the death and resurrection of Christ are made visible. Though it has enormous significance for the individual, baptism is celebrated communally, as the church pledges to uphold children in the faith, and as those baptized attest to their own (or future) faith. Baptism marks one's inheritance of the covenant: it is as much a sign of God's unending promise to covenant with a people as it is a testimony to that people's faith. Infant baptism is not an elixir for original sin, but a token of God's promise to children of the covenant.

To withhold the sacrament from infants and children, therefore, is tantamount to severing their lives from the church. In the face of any attempt to cut children off from the covenant, God's choice of children is irrevocable and irresistible: "God declares that he adopts our babies as his own before they are born, when he promises that he will be our God and the God of our descendants after us."[5] The language of adoption is explicit here and in other sections of the *Institutes,*[6] undermining any interpretation that would stress baptism as biological inheritance. We become heirs to God's promises in baptism not because of something we are, some innate connection to the divine, but because of God's gracious initiative. The family of God, at its core, is not the product of genetics, but of covenantal love and adoption.[7]

Because Calvin conceives baptism as an ecclesial practice, grounded in the church as the adoptive family of God, he explicitly rejects the surreptitious baptism of "unbelievers," a practice that had become prevalent in some corners of medieval Europe. In this vein, Calvin further clarifies his stance that baptism, by itself, is not necessary for salvation. In baptism, the community of faith and the parents pledge themselves to the child: "The children of believers are baptized not in order that they who were previously strangers to the church may then for the first time become children of God, but rather that, because by the blessing of the promise they already belonged to the body of Christ, they are received into the church with this solemn sign."[8] Children, for Calvin, are not anticipatory members of the community of faith; they already belong to it. The church recognizes this when it properly administers infant baptism as "something owed to them."[9] Calvin's baptismal theology thus encourages a stance that is rarely embodied in practice: children are as vital to the ongoing life of the covenant community as elders, pastors, and deacons. Children do not grow into participation in the worship, service, and life of the community, but partake of it and contribute to it from the first day of their lives.

Infant baptism not only signals the full membership of children in the covenant, it also entrusts them to others for nurture and instruction. "Being engrafted into the body of the church, [children] are somewhat more commended to the other members. Then, when they have grown up, they are greatly spurred to an earnest zeal for worshiping God, by whom they were received as children through a solemn symbol of adoption before they were old enough to recognize him as Father."[10] Calvin suggests that children come to the mysteries of Christian faith not as strangers, but as intimates in God's family, valued not for who they will become, but for who they are. The benefit of infant baptism also extends to each caregiver, teacher, and mentor: "For when we consider that immediately from birth God takes and acknowledges them as his children, we feel a strong stimulus to instruct them in an earnest fear of God and observance of the law."[11] In an age where concern for one's own family often results in claustrophobia—the isolation of nuclear families in gated communities where neighbors are strangers—Calvin's understanding of baptism explodes the idolatry of the nuclear family and locates us more securely in a family wider than we can imagine. In baptism, no child is left alone, but bound in security to others and the God who is Wholly Other. Infant baptism, in this sense, reminds us that security is not found in oneself.

Baptism points to a distinctive ecclesial ethic. By baptizing children, the community of faith expresses its hope that children will grow into awareness of God's claim upon them and confidently affirm the grace already given them. Baptism expresses what Milton Mayeroff describes as an ethic of care: "To care for another person, in the most significant sense, is to help him grow and actualize himself."[12] To grow into the knowledge that one is a child of the covenant is to be cared for, to become the person one is called to be. As the church cares for the children in its midst, moreover, its circle of care becomes larger. It cannot care for specific children without becoming caught up in the wider network of influences and factors—schools, neighborhoods, systems of income distribution—that have constructive and destructive impact on children's lives. In caring for particular children, the church that baptizes is drawn out of itself toward the children of the world.

In the face of multiple forms of violence that maim children's bodies, baptism is a powerful reminder that the Word not only becomes flesh, but that the Word *cares* for the flesh, and summons us to nurture all bodies. Barbara Pitkin draws out a striking implication of this sacrament that bathes the flesh. She asks, "How might present attitudes toward children's bodies (and especially the physical needs of poor children) be transformed and neglect and abuse of children challenged by taking seriously, with Calvin, the conviction that children bear in their very bodies the engravings of the divine covenant—that children's bodies are, in a sense, sacraments?"[13] Thus interpreted, baptism is a practice of vulnerability and resistance: In the former sense, it implies that we are claimed as heirs to the covenant in vulnerability, nakedness, and humility, just as a child comes into the world.[14] More significantly, baptism signals resistance to the world's violence that claims children's lives and scars children's bodies daily. By baptizing children, the church presents a viable alternative to systems of power that thrive on victimization. In the face of violence against children, the church does not resort to violence (and thus perpetuate its unending cycle), but names and claims children as heirs to the covenant. This promise is not grabbed by force, but inherited in vulnerability. By creating a space for children to be named and claimed, the church exposes the vacuous nature of power and violence, which in the end can bring only death. Here the Christian church makes a wager: that life is not found in a will to power, but in a vulnerable Savior who claims our vulnerable selves. By resisting violence with countercultural practice (creating space for children and upholding them in baptism), the church poses an alternative to the false "either-or" that often plagues our response to violence. By resorting neither to violent resistance nor passivity, the church stakes a claim (evidenced in baptism) with nonviolent resistance, foreshadowing an alternative order where children are already full members.[15] As baptism heralds the promise of the reign, the forgiveness of sin, and participation in the life of Jesus Christ, it also anticipates the healing of all children's bodies.

PEACEMAKING WITH CHILDREN

As the above interpretation of baptism suggests, one of the central liturgical practices of the Christian church is imbued with nonviolence. If Christians proclaim the good news of a nonviolent Savior, if the liturgy of the church is permeated with symbols of peace,[16] and if Christian eschatology points to a reign of justice and peace, then peacemaking is not peripheral to the ecclesia. Rather, the labor for peace is bound up with the nature of church and whom it proclaims as Savior. Laboring for something other than peace is a betrayal of the Gospel. As Stanley Hauerwas has written, "These rites, baptism and eucharist, are not just 'religious things' that Christian people do. They are the essential rituals of our politics. . . . For if the church *is* rather than has a social ethic, these actions are our most important social witness. It is in baptism and eucharist that we see most clearly the marks of God's kingdom in the world."[17] The peaceable reign is neither a timely word in an era of violence nor a romantic longing; rather, it is alternative orientation in a world ravaged by war and brutality: toward the Prince of Peace, who inaugurates a new reign.

The biblical witness is replete with imaginative depictions of the reign of peace, often placing children in surprising places. Consider Isaiah's description of the rule of the Davidic King:

> The wolf shall live with the lamb, the leopard shall lie down with the kid, the calf and the lion and the fatling together, and a little child shall lead them. The cow and the bear shall graze, their young shall lie down together; and the lion shall eat straw like the ox. The nursing child shall play over the hole of the asp, and the weaned child shall put its hand on the adder's den. (Isa. 11:6–8)

It is tempting to dismiss such images in our day as the longings of wartorn history: dreams where a nursing child and a toddler play with venomous snakes. Yet, the frequency of the image of children in biblical narrative suggests something else: peace, childhood, and vulnerability are not painful longings, but the way in which the God of Israel, the God of Jesus, reveals Godself. Not in majesty, but in humility and covenant; not in power, but in a vulnerability to power, even unto the cross; not in a self-made man, but in a poor child. In their bodies, in their vulnerability, children herald the peace that God gives.

The churches that have upheld this aspect of Christian proclamation most consistently trace their lineage to the Radical Reformation. Where other strands of the tradition have treated peace as a disposable commodity, Anabaptists suggest that to relinquish peacemaking is to deny Christ. J. Denny Weaver states the position succinctly: "Peace is not a nice ideal to be abandoned in the name of a higher good like national pride or the survival of capitalism or the institution of democracy. To people who follow Jesus, peace is a way of life which cannot be abandoned without abandoning him as well."[18] The church of Jesus Christ does not embody pacifism because peace marks the border between church and world, insulating those who are "in" from those who are "out"; rather, the church, as a herald of God's reign, announces and practices a peaceable kingdom in the world. Peacemaking, therefore, cannot rest in the ecclesia, but extends to others. In the end, peacemaking does not rest with the question of what reign we choose: that of church or that of the world? Rather, the practice of peacemaking signals the promise that God's reign embraces the *world* in peace. Caught up in this vision, the church cannot opt out of the world.

Laboring for peace in a violent world, however, places peacemakers in dangerous positions. The early Anabaptists lived in the midst of this peril with often devastating results. In the tumultuous saga of Reformation, Anabaptist communities of peace were perceived as threats to the gospel that could only be destroyed. Lutherans, Calvinists, and Roman Catholics all have ample blood on their hands, guilty of the crime of persecuting brothers and sisters whose response to the Gospel was not their own. Reformation era peacemakers took up the cause at the risk of their own lives, and many saw persecution as a sign of their faithfulness. Consider the words of Dietrich Philips, "Thus must the

true Christians here be persecuted for the sake of truth and righteousness, but the Christians persecute no one on account of his faith."[19]
Glimpsed in this light, the church is not a spiritual extension of a divinely ordained temporal order, but the prophetic challenge to violence, a prophecy that is enacted in the church's sacraments. The
church turns violence on its head by refusing the sword, celebrating and
proclaiming the sacrament of children's lives.

The turbid mix of violence, faith, and freedom runs especially thick
in the United States, where our national mythology draws sustenance
from a "good war" that brought about the nation's independence.
Weaver pinpoints this mythology with keen accuracy, seeing it lodged in
our educational system and political rhetoric. Children learn in school
that the wars that our nation fought (with the exception of Vietnam)
were all good: "War is the basis for freedom and . . . without war there
will not be freedom. . . . Deeply entrenched in the public mentality is the
notion that if the nation is to 'do something' about Saddam Hussein,
Somalia, Libya, terrorism, crime, or drugs, effective action implies the use
of guns or bombs. In the public mind, violence and freedom are tightly
bound together."[20] We now live in the wake of yet another "good war,"
bolstered by a presidential decree on the Axis of Evil and a benevolent
extension of freedom to the people of Iraq. During the conflict, however, accounts of Iraqi casualties were all but ignored, and it may be years
before we digest the enormity of loss. The practice of a nation that bol-
sters its rhetoric with the butt of a gun only serves to illuminate the
countercultural nature of peacemaking. To labor for peace is a practice
of vulnerability: on this issue our generation is no different than the
Reformation, or the early church. To work for peace is to stand out
from the bloodthirsty crowd. But when the wars of the earth devour the
lives of children, the Church of Jesus Christ can do nothing less. To become vulnerable for the cause of peace is to stand with children.

The temptation of the church, however, in practicing peacemaking
is that it equates itself with the reign Jesus proclaimed. When peacemaking is seen as the mark of the church that distinguishes it radically
from the world, the church both denies its complicity in the rising tides

of violence and proclaims that the *basilea* is realized only in its midst, instead of foreshadowing that reign in the world. That foretaste is witnessed when children are welcomed and nurtured in the faith as full members of the covenant, when the church offers its space and its life for homeless children, when the church urges conscientious objection to the wars that claim children's lives—wars fought with the blessing of the United States and the enrichment of our national coffers. The promise of the peaceable kingdom is a promise to the world's children: that regardless of their membership or status, God establishes peace and takes people, body and soul, as partakers of that peace.

The church is impelled to its mission of peacemaking because it is a community of the baptized. Just as the Word seeks flesh, so too does sacrament (the visible Word) pour out into the world in witness and action. If one way to understand baptism is as the church's welcome to the vulnerable, then baptismal life will extend beyond the church walls, laboring with all who are vulnerable and victimized by violence. The sacramental life of the church blossoms in its ethic of care for children, and will take root whenever children are welcomed, whenever their cause is supported, and whenever the church acts against the violence that plagues our streets. Such prophetic witness occurs wherever children are baptized, whenever children lead congregations in prayer, whenever the church throws itself as peacemaker into crucibles of struggle that claim children's lives. Practicing peace is one shape of the ecclesia. Drawing our life from the shape of this body will not provide a guarantee of success, if success is measured in how many we convert to the reign of peace. But drawing our life from it will nurture the lives of children touched by that reign, who may best understand that the Savior of the world comes to us as a child.

A SANCTUARY FOR CHILDREN

If the church's sacramental life issues forth in an ethic of care for children, announcing a reign of peace, then church also becomes a sanctuary for children.[21] In common parlance, sanctuary connotes retreat, a place to escape from the rough-and-tumble world, a haven for the battered and bruised. As critical as these dimensions of sanctuary are, they are stripped of prophetic potential if they are not connected to God's holiness: "In ancient Israel, a sanctuary was a place of special holiness where people worshiped. It was a place apart."[22] Sanctuary, in the first sense, is God's "dwelling-place" among us, charged with the grandeur of God, where the majesty of God's presence both empowers and over-whelms. A sanctuary is not our space; it belongs to God.

This same holy ground the church has honored as a refuge for soci-ety's victims. God's dwelling place is also a house for the dispossessed and despised, anyone on the run from powers that enslave and kill. If church is sanctuary, witnessing God's holiness and welcoming the vul-nerable go hand-in-hand. Eileen Lindner captures some of the history of the sanctuary movement: "The intention of sanctuary, legally speak-ing, grew in the twelfth century. In those days, one who was fleeing from someone who would do them harm could run into a church or monastery, ring the bell, and speak to the abbot. The abbot would pro-tect them for forty days, until the complaint could be adjudicated in some fair way." Drawing on this historical example, Lindner urges the contemporary church to consider itself a sanctuary for children. "Do our children not deserve forty days of shelter when they think they might be gay? When they're afraid of their schoolmates? When they don't have enough to eat? Or when they've been beaten?"[23] Glimpsed in this light, sanctuary is not primarily a comfort for middle-class es-capism, but an exigency of imperiled childhood. God's holy space is also the house of the orphan, the abused, and neglected.

The Hebrew prophets long recognized this surprising connection between the holy and the oppressed, going as far as to connect faithful-ness to the covenant with care for the orphan and widow (see chapter 2). For the prophets, one cannot privilege one over the other, as if recognition of God's holiness leads to care for the oppressed, or vice-versa. Rather, the insight is that offering a sanctuary for the oppressed is bound up with the holiness of God's dwelling-place. One does not show God reverence without simultaneously lifting up the downtrod-den; one does not really "care" with the vulnerable without recognizing that the holy God cares for all. Otherwise, our care rapidly degenerates into paternalism.

What are some characteristics of a church as sanctuary? At a bare minimum, the church would provide a place of physical and emotional safety. When children are threatened by violence (in school, home, and streets), the church models the ways of peace inaugurated in Christ's reign. Nursing the scars of violence can only take place if children's pain is heard, and if they are invited into the peaceable communion that promises the healing of human relationships. For children in the midst of adolescence, the church would also become a place where all questions are welcomed. Too often, the experience of many teenagers is that church is where the "answers" are dictated: answers about orthodox belief, about the "right" way to read the Bible, about sex (albeit in hushed and embarrassed tones). When the church offers answers without hearing children's questions, it is a wonder that more children do not opt out. If sanctuary is a model for church, however, then church becomes a place where children's questions are heard: where an eighth-grader's struggle to believe in God's goodness is taken seriously, where a sixteen-year-old can talk about her gay identity with the support of others, where a four-year-old can ask questions about whether Jesus was married without murmurs of adult laughter. The church, as a sanctuary for children, provides the space for physical safety and a harbor for emotional and spiritual growth, in the midst of God's holiness.

The church can sustain this sense of a spiritual harbor if it fosters children's participation in *all* facets of the church's ministry. In worship, the central act of ecclesial life, this is especially the case. A tendency among many mainline Protestant denomination is to set aside special times during worship particularly for children's benefit. Typically, this includes a children's sermon, where the young cavort down the aisles to the front of the sanctuary for a story and perhaps a few questions. While such moments are significant in recognizing children's attention spans and varied learning styles, they also can become exercises in to-kenism, particularly if children are shuttled out the doors after the sermon for time *away* from worship. In other cases, they become thin excuses for adult entertainment—where we can laugh at the ridiculous questions children ask the preacher. When we laugh at children, rather than with them, we tell them that they are not welcome at worship and replicate society's scorn for the youngest in our midst.

A church that welcomes the participation of children will not only set aside special times for children—such as children's sermons or having children come to the front of the congregation whenever baptisms occur—but will also nurture the voices of children in all facets of worship.[24] Children will offer prayers of confession, the post-communion prayer, minutes for mission, and, from time to time, even sermons.

Churches will not become sanctuaries if they only welcome and offer safety for the children within their walls. If the church is a genuine sanctuary for children, it will point to God's reign by protesting the violence that imperils children's lives and anticipating that reign in acts of healing. Its sanctuary embraces *all* children. A church that is a sanctuary will not only care for the homeless adolescents at its doorstep with food from its pantry, but also with acts of solidarity, such as providing counseling for youth, enabling them to return to school, conducting information campaigns about homeless children in the community, and marching with the homeless to the state capitol.

A sanctuary church draws its life not from itself, nor from its members, but from the promise of God's reign, which incorporates all children. Stephen Cherry writes that the church was enriched by the sanctuary movement of the 1980s—in the United States and Great Britain —where safety was provided within churches for political refugees (often in the face of immigration law).

> By making a sanctuary of a church, the building itself comes to symbolize a protest, and to be a reminder of the presence of injustice and division: 'the church as sanctuary comes to testify not to the presence of the kingdom-of-God but of its absence, its not-yet-hereness.' The church as sanctuary, in other words, witnesses *against* the notion that the sanctuary of God is a church building.[25]

Sanctuary is not a safety net for the comforted, but a response to the announcement of God's reign, extending the good news to the despised and the oppressed, even when such a response may contravene the laws of the state. In our time, perhaps the most vulnerable persons in our midst are illegal immigrant children. The "legal" response to their plight is to alert the INS and rally the deportation troops; the sanctuary announcement is to welcome that child and her family, to provide nurture and support for all children who come to our doors. If the church refuses to extend sanctuary and welcome to these children, it falls short of its call to be with the vulnerable, and becomes instead a club for the privileged.

In a nation characterized in recent times by the Patriot Act and xenophobia, sanctuary is even more urgent. Instead of constructing barriers to full participation in society and abetting the racial profiling of current post–September 11, 2001, lawmaking, the church becomes a sanctuary when it extends hospitality and grace to all, regardless of national origin. Sanctuary thus involves care for the marginalized and protest against policies that enforce marginalization. The life of the ecclesia results in an embrace of different children from around the world.

When the church becomes a sanctuary for childhood, it lives from the reign of God, journeying toward a future in God's hands. Jesus claims multiple times in the gospels that this reign belongs to children (Mark 10:14; Matt. 19:14; Luke 18:16). If we take that claim to heart, then a glimmer of God's reign will be reflected in the church's welcome, nurture, and shelter of children. As Anderson and Johnson write, "The church . . . lives according to the paradoxical belief that the fullness of humanity is to be found in struggling toward childhood. . . . The care of children itself is a window on what we believe."[26] As children are given sanctuary in our midst, they will offer prayers that call our renewed attention to their lives and the life of God's reign.

CHILDREN AND PRAYER

Prayer is a practice of vulnerability—prayer reminds us that we are not alone; we live in God's world. Though some popular conceptions stress solitude as fundamental to prayer, in actuality prayer is radically relational. In prayer, we recall our utter dependence on God, and by praying for and with others, we underscore the profound interconnections of human life. We cannot pray alone. By praying with others, we become open to them and bare ourselves to God. Children pray. When given the space, they will both mimic adults in prayer, but also branch out on their own, often voicing prayers that adults would dismiss as trivial: prayers of health for goldfish, of thanks for chocolate milk, of joy for squirrels. A church that baptizes, welcomes, and provides sanctuary for children will both teach children to pray and be taught by them.

The Heidelberg Catechism interprets the opening line of the Prayer of Our Savior with an eye to children. We are to pray "Our Father," so that "at the very beginning of our prayer he may awaken in us the childlike reverence and trust toward God which should be the motivation of our prayer."[27] The most recited Christian prayer recalls, from the outset, the trust and vulnerability of childhood. We pray not from positions of privilege and power, but in radical dependency on others. In the Christian tradition, the Word has abided as a central image: Word bespeaks creation into being, Word becomes flesh, Word is attested in Holy Scripture, Word is proclaimed from the pulpit and encountered in the sacraments, and Word comes to speak with us. God *speaks* and thus forges a relationship with a people. Prayer, in this sense, is our response to God, where our words are taken up by the divine Word. As God converses with us, we respond and listen as children join in the conversation.

The Shorter Catechism of the Westminster Confession offers another image for prayer: "Prayer is an offering up of our desires unto God, for things agreeable to his will, in the name of Christ, with confession of our sins, and thankful acknowledgment of his mercies."[28] In language rarely seen in theological texts, this confession focuses on *desire*. Prayers are not detached adult musings, but the earnest desires of a child. Most children are frank about their desires. When asked about Christmas, children will often concoct a laundry list of requests and desires. Yet prayer is not summarized by desire alone; it is the place where our desires are transformed and conformed to God's Word. Prayer, in this sense, provides the opportunity for growth in the Christian life— not so we outgrow our desires, but so our desires may be drawn out of ourselves toward the lives of others. Prayer connects us to others, to all who are vulnerable with us in the journey of faith.

Friedrich Schleiermacher, in a sermon on Jesus' prayer in Gethsemane, offers a similar conception of prayer. Recognizing that Jesus prayed out of longing and desire, "My Father, if it is possible, let this cup pass from me," Schleiermacher pays close attention to the prayer's conclusion, "yet not what I want but what you want" (Matt. 26:39b). Jesus' prayer is one of anguish and dependence, the agony of one who is about to be arrested and the trust of a child. For Schleiermacher, this prayer is a model for our own because it demonstrates how prayer changes *us*. We do not converse with God to placate God's demand for justice or to change God's mind. We pray in trust and thanksgiving, knowing that in prayer *we* are changed. "If our prayer has not the effect of moderating the wish that it expressed, of replacing the eager desire with quiet submission, the anxious expectation with devout calmness; then it was no true prayer."[29] Though Schleiermacher's exegesis quickly glosses over desire and replaces it with submission, his sermon is helpful in describing prayer as a process of growth, by which we are drawn deeper and deeper into God's very life. Is it not possible to construe this growth in a way that does not eliminate the desires of childhood but enriches them, so that these desires are connected to the desires for the well-being of all?

This widening of our desires, this calling us out of ourselves, is precisely what the Larger Catechism of the Westminster Confession highlights in its understanding of prayer. "For whom are we to pray? We are to pray for the whole church of Christ upon earth, for magistrates, and ministers, for ourselves, our brethren, yea, our enemies, and for all sorts of men living, or that shall live hereafter."[30] In sum, there is no place, no people that does not command our attention in prayer. In prayer, our desires are turned toward the desires of the whole world, in every age. Nothing is too trivial for prayer, nothing is beyond the pale of prayerful attention. Prayer widens our attention, awakens childlike desire and transforms it to the world's deepest needs and God's glory. A church that prays with children prays for all the world's children. In prayer, we rest in the assurance that God attends us.

I have been suggesting throughout this study that prayer is a distinct mode of attention, in which the self is drawn in compassion to God's world. As I noted in chapter 3, when given the opportunity children will pay attention, often in ways that defy the shortened attention spans of adults. Children attend with wonder to the minutiae of God's world: rocks, ferns, pill bugs, puddles. Ginny, a ten-year-old girl from Robert Coles' study, muses: "Maybe God puts you here and He gives you these hints of what's ahead, and you should pay attention to them, because that's Him speaking to you."[31] The people we meet, the puddles along our path, the unexpected events that no one can plan are summons for our attention. A church that prays with children will also be led by children during prayer. If church is a sanctuary, then children will not only read scripted prayers before the congregation, but will also voice prayers that are their own, using their words and images. If we listen to the prayers of children, we, too, can be changed. Just as the spoken prayer of one person summons the attention of the whole congregation, the prayer of a child can call us back to the wonder, desire, and pain of children in our world.

For the past three years, my daughter, Hannah Grace, has been praying: before dinner, before bedtime, and occasionally outside these appointed times of the day. Sometimes she prays in song, at other times with the spoken word; more recently she has begun offering what she calls "quiet prayers." As she folds her hands while lying in bed or clutches our hands around the dining room table, Hannah Grace utters nearly identical words every day: "Thank you for Shipe Park, all my friends, Mommy, Daddy, my school . . ." None of these prayers, doubtless, would be included in a contemporary devotional guide — the phrases are too simple and the concerns too mundane to make any spiritual bestseller list. Molly and I have told Hannah Grace that prayer is a way to talk with God, and she smiles when she hears this. I do not presume to know if she understands prayer; such presumption intrudes on a conversation that is uniquely hers. Yet in these prayers Hannah Grace pays attention to those people and things in her life that are most meaningful—the events and relationships that help form the person she is. Routine as these prayers are for her, they also reflect some of the ways in which my daughter's eyes are open to God's world, and the way the God who creates in love calls her to pay attention. If attention is a prerequisite to prayer, Hannah Grace lives her life strikingly *prayerfully*: Her life and prayers, moreover, are invitations for those who encounter them to live more attentively themselves.

Here we come full circle in our practices of vulnerability: baptizing children in the name of the Triune God, laboring for peace in a broken world, offering sanctuary to all who are vulnerable, the church prays for the world. Praying is never done in isolation, for in prayer we become vulnerable to the world, so that the cries of hungry children become our cries, so that the pain of an abused child is incorporated into the prayers of the community. Prayer connects us to others, and draws these connections into God's very life. The church is not only the church when it prays *for* children, but when it prays *with* children, when it allows their unique voices to become a part of the rich chorus of many. Being led by their voices, we return again to attentiveness in God's world and to the children who offer prayers.

One consequence of the Pauline metaphor of the church as the body of Christ, made up of many distinct members, is that God loves difference. The church is not a monotonal drone, but a veritable symphony of voices. Each voice is diminished if another voice is drowned out; each voice, in some way, is drawn into God's abundant life. The new life in Christ is not characterized by stultifying sameness, but by staggering diversity. The practices we have explored are some of the means by which we are opened to one another—in vulnerability and love—and opened to the God who becomes vulnerable for us. For too long, children have been considered on the fringes of the church's life as a worshipful, prayerful, sacramental, and peacemaking community. They have been welcomed, but chiefly at special times and places in the church's calendar and space. If I have suggested anything from following these practices of vulnerability in the church, children belong in the midst of the chorus. Without their voices, the church suffers and our attention is thrown back on ourselves. Paying attention to their voices —in baptism and prayer—the church is drawn out, as a prophetic witness in the midst of a world that often neglects and despises children. The hope of the world's children does not depend solely on the church (to claim as much exaggerates the church's significance and deflates the reign of God that it proclaims), but hope is present whenever the church becomes vulnerable for children's sake.

An ecclesiology that pays attention to childhood recognizes that children are not simply on their way to becoming members of the church and society. Instead, the church witnesses that children already are full heirs of the covenant community, who pray with desire. Childhood is not a waystation on the path to human becoming; it also informs the trajectory of one's entire life—lived with others, dependent on others, attentive of others. In this sense, we never leave childhood behind. The life of each child is already saturated with meaning, because the life of each child is part of the abundant diversity of God's world. Children matter not because of who they will *become*, but because of who they *are* and *whose* they are. To this theme we now turn, and to the gospel proclamation that we, too, are to become like children.

SIX

To Change and Become Like Children

eleology runs rampant in American consumer society. Human beings are always on the way somewhere, living into the future. Children receive this message from an early age, when they are peppered with adults' innocuous questions: "What do you want to be when you grow up?" "What will you do next year in school?" They ingest it in more pernicious forms when bombarded by advertising that claims they will become more adult-like if they wear these clothes or possess this bauble. To be sure, an emphasis on the future has its merits. Life is not simply one thing after another in the Christian schema, but the relentless lure of all things into the future of God's reign. The God who comes in Jesus Christ empowers us not only to live in the present, but redeems *all* time: past, present, and future. But teleology also has its dangers, and can disrupt the spontaneity and surprise of children's lives. If we conceive

children as only on the way to becoming something, we rob the present of its value and promise. If human life is viewed only in terms of an end, then those who do not reach it are emptied of God's creative intent. If teleology is the only determinant of human life, then the lives of children who die before becoming adults are devoid of meaning.

Karl Rahner criticizes the tendency in postindustrial societies to view human life as a sequence of stages that we subsequently outgrow: "We conceive of our personal lifespan as the sum total of a series of phases in life, each of which as it is exhausted leads on to the next, the very meaning of which is to disappear into the next, to be a preparation for it, to 'exist' for the further stages beyond itself. Above all we conceive of youth and childhood in this sense."[1] According to this model, children are inundated with the importance of growing up into the real world of adult responsibilities. Though childhood may be valued as a stage of life, little of it is carried over into young adulthood once we leave childhood behind. We are children only for a time.

In the face of a society that places a high premium on "growing up," on becoming the kind of consumers that adults are,[2] I close this study with an obvious, yet underappreciated claim: children already are fully alive, fully present, fully endowed with promise in God's world. They do not simply grow into the future, but inhabit a present fully pregnant with meaning.

In interpreting children's lives, two myths have captivated Christians' attention, both of which are rampant in North American society. One is the myth of childhood innocence, of children who come into the world sheltered and protected from the world and its evils. The damage wrought on children's lives is solely the result of societal influence, particularly in its urban manifestations. If children could only flee the cities and cavort in the countryside, we could preserve the exuberance and unblemished life of the child. From Rousseau to the Boy Scouts to Peter Pan, the myth that the child is perfect and that the world is the source of all evil has been captivating. The goal is to become a child again, and escape the realm of noxious adulthood in order to become a more responsible adult. The problem with this myth is that it renders children passive vessels, blank slates upon which society impresses destructive or constructive messages that determine the child's future. In this model children are stripped of agency: the becoming that they undergo is not the complex result of being actors and acted upon, but the sheer result of adult imposition. No wonder Peter Pan wanted to escape this world!

On the other hand are even more damaging interpretations of childhood that are indifferent to children or blame children for their own predicaments. Whether encountered in injunctions to "beat the sin" out of children, in interpretations of sin that consider childhood the root of all selfishness, or in economic systems that consider children unproductive citizens, these interpretations leave children on the margins. Children, in this sense, need to become adults rather quickly and leave childhood behind as an obstacle for others to surmount.

The interpretation of childhood that I have been offering is more complex than either one of these alternatives suggests: the vulnerability of childhood conveys something of what it means to be created in God's image, that vulnerability underscores the relationality of human life and exposes the scars of violence within it, that children experience sin both in terms of acting and being acted upon, that intimations of the reign of God are witnessed whenever the church displays practices of vulnerability inherent to its life. Childhood, in this sense, is a two-way street. Children grow into adulthood, but adults also learn from children. Each stage of human life is precious and valuable in its own right, not in terms of what it precedes, but as God elects all stages of human life. On this reading, if children are those who are beginning the life of graced difference that God calls us to embody, adults also "become like" children when they open themselves to the difference that God creates. In response to the violence that imperils children's lives, the hope for children's future rests in possibilities of an alternative vision, epitomized in the gospel's unique reversal of children and adults. With this in mind, we turn to two pivotal stories of Jesus with children and spell out some of their implications for childhood as a basic condition of graced human life in God's diverse world.

JESUS AND THE CHILDREN

> At that time the disciples came to Jesus and asked, "Who is the greatest in the kingdom of heaven?" He called a child, whom he put among them, and said, "Truly I tell you, unless you change and become like children, you will never enter the kingdom of heaven. Whoever becomes humble like this child is the greatest in the kingdom of heaven. Whoever welcomes one such child in my name welcomes me. (Matt. 18:1–5)

> People were bringing little children to him in order that he might touch them; and the disciples spoke sternly to them. But when Jesus saw this, he was indignant and said to them, "Let the little children come to me; do not stop them; for it is to such as these that the kingdom of God belongs. Truly I tell you, whoever does not receive the kingdom of God as a little child will never enter it." And he took them up in his arms, laid his hands on them, and blessed them. (Mark 10:13–16)

Stories of Jesus with children have captured the attention of Christians across the ages. In the present era, they tend toward the sentimental: images of a placid Galilean in a bucolic setting, blessing cherub-faced babes while resting under an olive tree. There is no doubt that Jesus welcomes children in these texts, and that his welcome, blessing, and suggestion of children as models confounds the outlook of his audience. Yet the tendency toward the sentimental minimizes the subversive nature of these narratives. In these texts Jesus does not romanticize children by extolling their innocence in his embrace, but heralds the reorientation of God's reign. The texts, in other words, do not uplift a placid ideal of childhood, but signal a renewed attention to children, a care for children, because the new reign belongs to them. Both pericopes of Jesus with children fall in line with his ministry to outcasts and nobodies that disrupts the present age. The Galilean who dines with the unclean, the Prince of Peace who touches the untouchable, the carpenter who uplifts the poor, is also the One who blesses children. Jesus' ministry to the outcasts here comes full circle, extending hospitality to those who are only "on their way" to becoming full persons. When the disciples argue about greatness and when they seek to bar children from coming to him, Jesus welcomes the children and becomes indignant with those who would exclude them.

Attempts to interpret these passages are legion. In some eras, allegory ruled: Jesus' blessing is less a gesture of hospitality to children than it is a blessing of the child-like nature of mature persons of faith. Such interpretations, however, obscure the children of the narrative and overlook the extensive ethical demands of Jesus' words. In this regard, numerous contemporary interpretations of the texts examine the status of children in the Mediterranean world of the first century. Since infanticide and exposure[3] were common practice in many quarters of the Hellenistic world, these texts offer an explicit rejection of the marginal status of children and a resounding affirmation of their character as full human persons. Such interpretations are all the more persuasive when one recognizes the Jewish roots of Jesus' teaching. Indeed, first-century Judaism issued some of the most vigorous polemics against Gentile practice regarding children, echoed in Israel's recognition of children as members of the covenant community. In this reading, when Jesus tells the disciples to "become like children," he is pointing less to their inner nature than to their *status* and how they regard status: those on the outside come first, the lowly will sit in the place of honor. This reversal of status, in turn, compels the disciples to care for the vulnerable and victimized—for it is to such as these that God's reign belongs.

If the texts pointed to status alone, however, one wonders why the identification of the reign with a child. Yes, children were marginal in the Mediterranean world and they continue to occupy that space today. But do the stories of Jesus with children only present children as faceless representatives of marginality? If Jesus calls to children, takes them in his arms, and urges his audience to become like children, then do the stories also suggest something about children, some aspect of their nature that others recall? This possibility is all the more striking if we recognize how anomalous the idea of children as *models* for adults was even in a Jewish context. Highlighting Jesus' claim, "Whoever does not receive the kingdom of God as a little child will never enter it" (Mark 10:15), Judith Gundry-Volf writes, "Nowhere in Jewish literature are children put forward as models for adults, and in a Greco-Roman setting, comparison with children was highly insulting."[4] Obviously, Jesus does not specify abstract qualities of childhood—such as openness, vulnerability, trust, or dependence—but welcomes children and takes them in his arms. This embrace, however, is an embrace of children who portray aspects of discipleship that the twelve are to embody. Something about childhood itself intimates faithful following of Jesus Christ.

A full analysis of these texts focuses on both the *status* of children (and our responsibility to welcome, care for, and protect children) as well as the *nature* of children (who represent something about discipleship that we can emulate). We will revisit the question of welcoming children at the close of this chapter. The nature of children, however, appears elusive. As the early sections of this book have demonstrated, there is no singular essence of childhood, no such creature as a model child. Yet children do exhibit degrees of the differently constituted relationality and vulnerability that human life entails. In this sense, the openness of children, the vulnerability of children, the trust of children, becomes a window on what it means to be created in God's image. The children who are rejected by others (whether by first-century disciples or twenty-first-century consumers), are the inheritors of God's reign. Gundry-Volf's analysis broaches this connection between the status and nature of children: "Entering the reign of God 'as a child' thus seems to involve *both* a certain status—actual dependence on God—*and* a corresponding quality—trust—that are both 'childlike.'"[5] In this sense, children enflesh discipleship in ways that defy a teleologically oriented Christian life. They are not on the way to becoming disciples, but already are disciples in ways that we cannot fully fathom.

BECOMING LIKE A CHILD?

If we take seriously the suggestion that children can model something about discipleship for us, does that imply a conversion on the part of adults? Jesus' blunt saying, "unless you *change* and become like children," suggests as much. Yet, this change seems insulting in our day, where behaving like a child rings like an accusation and an avoidance of responsibility. What would becoming like a child resemble? The escape of Peter Pan? The wail of a baby? The curiosity of a preschooler? Drawing on a suggestive essay by Karl Rahner, I suggest that becoming like a child implies our partnership with God, in frank admission of the vulnerability and brokenness of human life. To become like a child, in this sense, is to become who we already are—the full inheritors of God's blessing and election of us, valued not for who we will become, but for whose we already are.

Rahner begins his essay with a claim that has reverberated throughout the preceding pages: "Right from the beginning [the child] is already in possession of that value and those depths which are implied in the name of a person. It is not simply that he gradually grows into a person. He *is* a person. . . . The child is the person who is, right from the first, the partner of God."[6] With characteristic grace, Rahner traces the contours of a theology of childhood by considering children as full *persons* and *partners* with God. The theme of personhood has permeated this analysis of childhood; partnership has played a less prominent role. Recalling the interpretation of election that was developed in chapter 3, an expansion of Rahner's understanding of partnership emphasizes that we are partners of God not because of something we accomplish or embody, but because God chooses us. We do not make ourselves partners with God; God takes us as we are, names us, and makes us participants in God's very life. This understanding of partnership may have particular resonance with infants, with those persons who—in the eyes of modern psychology and economics—are prior to the age of full human agency. If infants, too, are God's partners, this implies that partnership is not something we create. Partnership is God's endeavor, not ours, and we stand in the light of that divine initiative.

In a broken world, however, children already participate in the alienating and destructive rifts that scar the planet. Though they participate at first unwittingly, they are by no means immune from the cancer of sin. "Christianity views even childhood as already and inevitably the origin precisely of that man to whom guilt, death, suffering and all the forces of bitterness in human life belong as conditions of his very existence."[7] In this recognition, however, do we not run the risk of invoking the model of childhood I have warned against consistently: namely, the child as the locus of sin? Perhaps, if this is the only chord that we emphasize. Rahner's work, however, offers an important caveat: sin occurs within the larger context of God's unmerited grace. The brokenness of human life always proceeds within the very life of God. Though sin looms large, God's grace is more immense. The initial word in the cosmos (and the final word) is not the brokenness and violence that we engender, but the pulse of God's love that courses through the universe. Recalling our previous discussion of sin, we recognize that sin, from a child's perspective, is as much about experiencing rejection and violence as it is about inflicting violence on others. To become like a child is to open one's eyes again to the violence that surrounds us, but also to fall into the arms of God's grace, the God who experiences the violence that scars the earth and announces a final word of peace.

We tend toward theological reductionism if we consider children only as innocent or only as sinful. Rahner suggests that childhood itself might best be described as a *mystery*, an insight that has enormous merit, since it refuses to typecast children and claims that children, from the beginning, are enormously varied creatures who confound theological typology. This embrace of mystery is another aspect of becoming a child again:

> Hence, too, provided we reverently and lovingly preserve this state of being delivered over to the mystery, life becomes for us a state in which our original childhood is preserved for ever; a state in which we are open to expect the unexpected, to commit ourselves to the incalculable, a state which endows us with the power still to be able to play, to recognize that the powers presiding over existence are greater than our own designs, and to submit to their control as our deepest good.[8]

The mystery of human life is that our lives are given over to God, the creator and sustainer of the universe. Children, Rahner claims, are open to mystery, in part because of their capacity to expect what cannot be expected, to dream what cannot be dreamed, and to be willing to admit that they do not supply the final power in the universe. Though his focus on submission ignores some problems (often the "greater power" that adults instruct children to submit to are the fists of abuse), Rahner's account is fundamentally relational. Children, from the beginning, are aware of human relationality in the caress of loving arms and the soothing notes of a lullaby. To submit to the power of life in relation (not death and abuse), to recognize that we are not alone, is to embrace mystery.

The life of the world's children resists commodification. The mystery of their lives becomes manifest not in stultifying sameness, but in surprising heterogeneity. These themes of childhood are grounded in the mystery of the Triune God who creates in difference. The God who relates in difference (Creator, Christ, and Holy Spirit), graces creatures who reflect, however dimly, relationality-in-difference. No one child is like another; yet each is related, however remotely, to every other child. Because each child brings a different story to the tapestry of creation, there is no way to describe the totality of childhood. Yet one response to the God who creates in freedom is to listen to as many of their stories as possible, to be changed by their different refrains and opened to those children anew.

To become a child is not to revert to immaturity, nor is it to escape the responsibilities and obligations of the adult world. As the beginning of graced human life-in-difference, childhood abides when we are open to the partnership God gives, when we affirm the vulnerability and difference of others, when we are drawn toward each other in relationships of care and are open to the mystery of life itself. Rather than something we outgrow, childhood "endures as that which is given and abiding, the time that has been accepted and lived through freely. Childhood does not constitute past time, time that has eroded away, but rather that which remains."[9] Anyone who has spent a significant length of time with young children will recognize how quickly they subvert our linear understanding of time.[10] Few instances demonstrate this subversion more than play. Children do not play to accomplish something, but for the joy of the moment. In the immediacy of child's play, the future has little bearing: what matters is the awareness that right here, right now, I am delighting with my playmates. Children certainly can conceive of past and future as well, but in the immediacy of a child's world, time is fulfilled in the joy and grace of each moment. To delight in the life given to us by God is certainly a faithful response to the God who creates in God's image. We encounter such delight whenever we play with the children in our midst who open us to the tapestry of their lives and, however momentarily, to the fulfillment of all time. In Rahner's words, "We only *become* the children who we were because we gather up time —and in this our childhood too—into our eternity."[11] In this sense, to become like children is to become who we already are.[12]

WELCOMING CHILDREN IN JESUS' NAME

At one level, Jesus' injunction to change and become like children is a call to conversion. Becoming like children is a process of self-discovery, not because of the efforts we undertake, but because we live in response to the God who bestows all things with life. Becoming a child, in this sense, is something that God accomplishes in us. Yet this conversion can become suffocating if it only causes us to discover ourselves anew. To become a child is not simply to discover our individual lives, but also to be drawn toward others, indeed, bound together with others. As Jesus' gestures in these stories demonstrate, becoming a child involves the blessing, embracing, and welcoming of children threatened by violence. To discover our childhood is also to be claimed by the children that surround us. Matthew is emphatic about this point: welcoming one child in Jesus' name is equivalent to welcoming Jesus (18:5). Discipleship takes flesh. If a child models discipleship, welcoming children is an outgrowth of following Jesus; indeed, if we do not welcome children we cannot claim that we are following the Risen Lord.

Judith Gundry-Volf interprets this command to welcome children as Jesus' identification of his ministry with the status of children: "*The child thus represents Jesus as a humble, suffering figure.* Welcoming the child signifies receiving Jesus and affirming his divinely given mission as the suffering Son of Man."[13] Jesus Christ reveals himself in the humble and lowly. The echoes with other statements of Jesus resound here: "For I was hungry and you gave me food, I was thirsty and you gave me something to drink, I was a stranger and you welcomed me, I was naked and you gave me clothing, I was sick and you took care of me, I was in prison and you visited me" (Matt.25:35–6). What these sayings suggest is that Jesus is present—yea incarnated—in the vulnerable children in our midst. Likewise, our hospitality for the vulnerable is a demonstration of our discipleship. To be claimed by children is to welcome the child born in a Bethlehem stable.

One critique of this theological claim is that it invariably obscures the particularity of the children we welcome. If every welcome of children is actually a welcoming of Christ, then the child is significant only as s/he embodies Christ. Such a principle may have the unintended effect of clouding our vision to the particular injuries and vulnerabilities of each child, leaving us smug in a vague comfort that Christ is the one we are really welcoming. The texts, however, are emphatic in affirming the particularity of each child. In Matthew 18, Jesus calls a child and places that child in the disciples' midst. In Mark 10, Jesus blesses children and takes them in his arms. His actions call our attention to *particular* children, not to some vague idea of childhood. The face of Jesus Christ and the unique face of each child are not mutually exclusive. Indeed, following Christ is one way of becoming open to the abundant difference of children in the world; beholding their faces, we come face-to-face with the Savior again. The faces of each—Jesus and the child—become more visible in connection with each other.

In these texts, welcoming children does not occur under any circumstances. Just as Jesus' actions call our attention to the unique faces of children in our midst, the welcoming of children occurs in the specific name of Jesus. If Jesus unveils the particularity of each child of God, the church's care of children illumines the particularity of the Annointed One of God. These reciprocal gestures are all the more significant in an age such as ours where hospitality has become diluted and sentimental, or even a thin guise for marginal acceptance of others without being claimed by their difference. Where welcoming gays and lesbians in congregations translates into a denial of their calling to ministry and a dismissal of same-sex partnerships; where welcoming the homeless means a remote corner of the church building may be reserved for "their" use; where extending hospitality to children means removing them from worship and whisking them away to a dingy and cluttered room, the hospitality of Jesus' name is not extended. When tokenism or provisional acceptance occurs, our welcome is fraudulent. Such "welcomes" do not occur in the name of the One who was claimed by others.

Welcoming in the name of Jesus is not simply an evangelistic tool. The name of Jesus itself does not bolster one's privilege or legitimate one's status as a disciple. To welcome in the name of Jesus is not the spouting of a slogan that smothers the particularity of other names. Rather, to name Jesus in acts of hospitality and care is to be caught up in the entire trajectory of Jesus' ministry. To speak his name is to be drawn into the *way* of Jesus Christ: a way of vulnerable love made real in the flesh that opens us radically to others. This is not a way of privilege, superiority, and trumpeting exclusion, but covenant, vulnerability, and difference. To welcome in the name of Jesus means that others have a claim *on us.* If we welcome children in this name, they become not simply the recipients of our care, but guides along the way. Care of children, in this sense, allows us not simply to become who we already are, it also clarifies our confession of Jesus as Savior and points to the inbreaking of God's reign among us. Considered in this manner, the church's attention to children has anthropological implications (clarifying who we are), Christological consequences (clarifying who Christ is), and profound ecclesial dimensions (pointing to a church where all children have a voice).

Jesus' embrace of children is thus a judgment on the present world, where children are threatened and scarred by violence. In Gundry-Volf's words, "Jesus did not just teach how to make an adult world kinder and more just for children; he taught the arrival of a social world in part defined by and organized around children. He cast judgment on the adult world because it is not the child's world."[14] Jesus' word of judgment is at the same time a gesture of hope. In response to disciples who discouraged others in bringing children to Jesus, in the face of arguments about greatness that have no time for children, Jesus turns our attention to the youngest in their midst. His naming and blessing of specific children in the face of powers that exclude and ignore children is testament to the hope that each child brings to the world. To name and care for children is both to reject the death-dealing structures of power and violence that serve only the interests of the supposedly invulnerable, and to suggest that these structures do not have the final word. Just as Jesus took children in his arms, the church is called to touch whatever children come its way: no matter where they are from, no matter when they come. Part of the hope of the world's children, and the world itself, rests with those courageous enough to adopt practices of vulnerability and care that extend to all who are rejected and despised.

Christians have long proclaimed that the hope of the world comes with a baby born in Bethlehem. Hope, for Christians, comes in the name of a child, a name that opens our lives to the presence of all children and the claim they have upon us. The way of Jesus Christ is not a way unto privilege, but a way of solidarity with the least, a way that opens us to others. In a world where children are ignored, excluded, and abused, the way of Jesus leads us to the lives of children. As those who are not "on the way" to personhood, but already embody the vulnerability and relationality of the *imago Dei,* children call us back to who we are, and how we structure our lives. To live with children is not easy: working with children tries patience as much as it heightens joy. Moreover, the threats that imperil children's lives—from famine, war, poverty, and the sex trade—are overwhelming. Yet the final word of the cosmos is not the violence that destroys lives, but the coming of the Christ child again, the One who announces the peaceable reign, where children will play once again in the streets, place their hands over the adder's den, and lead the people home. In the meantime, while the violence that threatens children's lives rages, we anticipate this reign whenever, by God's grace, we turn toward children, are changed by their faces, and become vulnerable with them for the sake of their lives and the One who gives them life.

Notes

PREFACE

1. McFague's recent work, *Life Abundant: Rethinking Theology and Economy for a Planet in Peril* (Minneapolis: Fortress Press, 2001), 25–37, offers an excellent example of how advocacy theology matters for creaturely well-being in God's world.

2. I will explore these threats to children's lives more fully in chapter 4.

3. The phrase "what I am not" comes from a recent article by Deanna Thompson, "Teaching What I'm Not: Embodiment, Race, and Theological Conversation in the Classroom," *Teaching Theology & Religion* 3, no. 3 (2000). Thompson writes, "Human beings embody multiple identities, which cannot be neatly divided one from another and analyzed individually." Ibid., 167.

CHAPTER 1

1. We will explore this connection further, by examining Christian baptism in chapter 5.

2. Judith M. Gundry-Volf, "The Least and the Greatest: Children in the New Testament," in *The Child in Christian Thought,* ed. Marcia J. Bunge (Grand Rapids: Wm. B. Eerdmans, 2001), 35.

3. Multiple episodes in the Hebrew Bible can be read as narratives of barrenness that are resolved through God's gift of children, who are signs of God's favor. The stories of Sarah, Rebekah, Rachel, and Hannah revolve around long-anticipated births of children that evoke outbursts of joy and implicit identifications of God's favor. Jeanne Stevenson-Moessner writes of these narratives, "The throbbing womb of a loving and tender God overcomes the curse of barrenness in all its many guises." *The Spirit of Adoption: At Home in God's Family* (Louisville: Westminster John Knox Press, 2003), 22. Stevenson-Moessner also highlights the problematic implications of these narratives for women and couples who struggle with infertility today. Because each of these stories overcomes "barrenness" with the miraculous birth of a child, "there is not one model, mentor, or mother in Scripture with whom modern-day infertile women can connect." Ibid., 23.

4. This test also appears in modified form in the New Testament Letter of James. "Religion that is pure and undefiled before God, the Father, is this: to care for orphans and widows in their distress, and to keep oneself unstained by the world" (James 1:27).

5. John Calvin develops his theology of baptism along decidedly covenantal lines, with analogous implications for the membership of children in the church and the church's care for children. We will explore these themes in chapter 5.

6. Though strong doctrines of original sin have sometimes led to harsh disciplinary measures against children (New England Puritanism is one example), more optimistic anthropologies may prove equally abusive of children's lives. The foolish child, according to the optimist, represents an "aberration" who must be reformed by the rod. Bonnie Miller-McLemore writes, "There is not a one-to-one correlation be-

tween ideas about original sin and harsh punishment of children." *Let the Children Come: Reimagining Childhood from a Christian Perspective* (San Francisco: Jossey-Bass, 2003), 65. Miller-McLemore's work offers one of the most illuminating contemporary reflections on children and sin, which we will encounter in chapter 4.

7. Augustine, *Confessions*, trans. R. S. Pine-Coffin (New York: Penguin Books, 1961), 27–8.

8. Ibid., 28. Miller-McLemore offers a more irenic read of Augustine: "Both my husband and I saw something akin to what Augustine described once a new baby brother entered our family. . . . Over the years I have witnessed acts of meanness among my sons and their peers . . . that seem to have no other obvious source besides the sheer pleasure of the shabby act itself." *Let the Children,* 63. Augustine's articulation of sin, on this read, does not blame "innocent" infants, but points to selfish propensities in human behavior that emerge remarkably early in childhood.

9. According to Vigen Guroian, "Chrysostom maintains that newborn infants are innocents, wholly without sin. Infants may belong to a corporate human nature, which in its wholeness is mortally wounded by original sin and the will of which is weakened and prone to personal sin, but they are still innocents." "The Ecclesial Family: John Chrysostom on Parenthood and Children," in Bunge, *The Child in Christian Thought,* 70.

10. John Crysostom, "An Address on Vainglory and the Right Way for Parents to Bring Up Their Children," in *Christianity and Pagan Culture in the Later Roman Empire,* ed. M.L.W. Laistner (Ithaca, NY: Cornell University Press, 1967), 99–100.

11. In fact, Luther celebrated childhood, and called his own children God's "little jesters" as they played about his feet while he worked. See Walther von Loewenich, *Martin Luther: The Man and His Work,* trans. Lawrence W. Denef (Minneapolis: Augsburg, 1986), 285.

12. Martin Luther, "Treatise on Good Works," in *Selected Writings of Martin Luther: 1517–1520,* ed. Theodore G. Tappert (Philadelphia: Fortress Press, 1967), 164, emphasis mine.

13. In some instances Luther's words are harsh: "If you are unwilling to obey father and mother or submit to them, then obey the hangman; and if you will not obey him, then obey the grim reaper, Death!" "The Large Catechism," in *The Book of Concord,* ed. Theodore G. Tappert (Philadelphia: Fortress Press, 1959), 383.

14. Jean Jacques Rousseau, *Émile,* trans. William H. Payne (New York: D. Appleton and Company, 1908), 1.

15. Ibid., 24.

16. Ibid., 85.

17. In the spectrum of Christian thought, nineteenth- and twentieth-century "liberalism" is analogous to Rousseau on some matters. Horace Bushnell, for example, interprets sin socially, and suggests that children come "into the world not morally perfect, but morally innocent." Margaret Bendroth, "Horace Bushnell's *Christian Nurture,*" in Bunge, *The Child in Christian Thought,* 361. See also Horace Bushnell, *Christian Nurture* (New York: Charles Scribner's Sons, 1908), 90–122. The revisionist Catholic "creation spirituality" of Matthew Fox rejects Augustinian anthropology and claims that each child's "earthiness" is its original blessing. Matthew Fox, *Original Blessing: A Primer in Creation Spirituality* (Santa Fe, NM: Bear & Company, 1983), 57–65; 117–25.

18. Rousseau, *Émile,* 62.

19. The recent U.S. phenomenon of trying juvenile offenders as adults, however, represents a marked departure from this understanding of childhood.

20. Thomas Aquinas, *Summa Theologiae* (Cambridge: Blackfriars, 1964), II–II.10.12.

21. Ibid.

22. Ibid., I–II.89.6.

23. Ibid.

24. Ibid., II–II.4.4.

25. I will explore the following two pericopes more fully in chapter 6. See also Miller-McLemore, *Let the Children,* 94–104.

26. Even the suggestion to welcome children in Jesus' name can become an excuse for avoiding the realities of children's lives. On some

readings of the Matthean text, what is critically important is that one welcome *Jesus*. The child, as the means by which the Savior is welcomed, is obscured by the naming of Jesus. A close reading of the text, however, yields different results: paying close attention to children is to welcome Jesus. One cannot welcome Jesus without beholding the detail and hearing the claims of the children we encounter.

CHAPTER 2

1. For a compelling argument that human persons are defined not by some common essence they possess, but by the differences that mark their lives under God, see Ian McFarland's *Difference & Identity* (Cleveland: Pilgrim Press, 2001).

2. For a survey of how the *imago Dei,* narrowly translated as power, has abetted environmental devastation, see Jürgen Moltmann, *God in Creation*, trans. Margaret Kohl (Minneapolis: Fortress Press, 1993), 20–52, and Sallie McFague, *The Body of God* (Minneapolis: Fortress Press, 1993), 1–25.

3. Karl Barth, *The Humanity of God,* trans. John Newton Thomas (Philadelphia: John Knox Press, 1960), 51.

4. For example, Isaiah compares the relationship between God and Israel with a bridegroom and bride (Isa. 62:5); in Jeremiah, God is compared with a mother who laments over her children (Jer. 10:19–21).

5. See James Evans' *We Have Been Believers* (Minneapolis: Fortress Press, 1992), 33–52, for an excellent discussion of the subversion of facile distinctions between "insiders" and "outsiders."

6. For a more detailed analysis of these dimensions of Jesus' ministry, see David H. Jensen, *In the Company of Others* (Cleveland: Pilgrim Press, 2001), 74–80.

7. John Dominic Crossan, *Jesus: A Revolutionary Biography* (San Francisco: HarperCollins, 1994), 82.

8. Jesus' interaction with lepers brings to mind current stigmas and stereotypes that surround persons with HIV/AIDS in contemporary American society. Like no other disease, HIV/AIDS evokes ridicule, hatred, scorn, and blame, simply because of societal prejudice.

9. Infections diseases continue to affect children at alarming rates. Twenty-seven percent of children worldwide are not immunized against any diseases, and 9 percent die by the age of five. Unicef, *The State of the World's Children 2002* (New York: Unicef, 2002), 13. In a broken world, children suffer the scourge of disease on a disproportionate scale.

10. Anselm, "Why God Became Man," in Eugene R. Fairweather, ed., *A Scholastic Miscellany: Anselm to Ockham* (Philadelphia: Westminster Press, 1956), 142.

11. Ibid., 161.

12. Hegel, *Lectures on the Philosophy of Religion,* vol. 3, ed. Peter C. Hodgson (Berkeley: University of California Press, 1985), 323.

13. William C. Placher, *Narratives of a Vulnerable God* (Louisville: Westminster John Knox, 1994), 15.

14. Alan E. Lewis has documented this absence in theological reflection rather astutely and offers, in a posthumously published work, an arresting theology of Holy Saturday. He argues that Saturday offers the neglected space for a more thorough understanding of Christ's death and resurrection. See Lewis, *Between Cross and Resurrection* (Grand Rapids: Wm. B. Eerdmans, 2001), especially 69–129.

15. Johann Baptist Metz, *Faith in History and Society,* trans. David Smith (New York: Crossroad, 1980), 128.

16. For further reflections on Christ's resurrection as "absent presence" see Jensen, *In the Company of Others,* 108–30.

17. The traditional language of Father, Son, and Holy Spirit is fraught with dangers of its own: patriarchal images that often reinforce problematic understandings of a distant deity rather than the vulnerable God of incarnation. I call attention to the idolatrous implications of such language, and will use it interchangeably with other Trinitarian formulations, such as Creator, Christ, Holy Spirit, fully aware that many alternatives have modalistic implications. It is my deepest hope that the church in the coming centuries may find richer, alternative language for expressing Trinitarian wisdom. Such efforts, of course, will come not from theologians alone, but from the wellspring of worshipping communities themselves.

18. S. Mark Heim, *The Depth of the Riches: A Trinitarian Theology of Religious Ends* (Grand Rapids: Wm. B. Eerdmans, 2001), 171, 174.

19. Shirley Guthrie, *Christian Doctrine,* rev. ed. (Louisville: Westminster John Knox, 1994), 92.

20. Heim, *Depth of the Riches,* 126.

21. Thornton Stringfellow, quoted in Evans, *We Have Been Believers,* 36. In the present century, Princeton philosopher Peter Singer has argued that parents have the right to kill severely cognitively impaired babies, because they are not yet full persons. See Harriet McBryde Johnson, "Unspeakable Conversations or How I Spent One Day as a Token Cripple at Princeton University," *New York Times Magazine,* Feb. 16, 2003: 50–79.

22. Placher, *Narratives,* xiii.

CHAPTER 3

1. The idea of the child as a "metaphor of hope" comes from a recent article by Jürgen Moltmann, "Child and Childhood as Metaphors of Hope," *Theology Today* 56, no. 4 (2000): 592–603.

2. Delores Williams, *Sisters in the Wilderness* (Maryknoll, NY: Orbis Books, 1993), 5.

3. Ibid., 31.

4. One of the striking aspects of Genesis 16 is Hagar's naming of God, El-roi. "Hagar is the only person in the Bible to whom is attributed the power of naming God." Ibid., 23.

5. Ibid., 33.

6. See J. Milburn Thompson, *Justice & Peace: A Christian Primer* (Maryknoll, NY: Orbis, 1997), 30.

7. Margaret Bendroth notes: "Many historians have documented the gradual transformation of domestic arrangements between the eighteenth and nineteenth centuries, from large socially embedded households to smaller, more self-contained family units—a form that maximized each child's share of parental devotion. . . . Unlike their counterparts among the working and immigrant poor, they had no real economic function; they were, in a sense, the psychological and spiritual 'projects' of their parents."

"Children of Adam, Children of God: Christian Nurture in Early Nineteenth-Century America," *Theology Today* 56:4 (Jan. 2000): 500.

8. McFarland, *Difference & Identity,* 8.

9. Ibid., 1.

10. Ibid., 28.

11. John Calvin, *Institutes* (1559) 3.21.7.

12. Karl Barth, *Church Dogmatics,* IV.1, G. W. Bromiley and T. F. Torrance, eds. (Edinburgh: T. & T. Clark, 1956), 39.

13. Calvin, *Institutes,* 3.22.2.

14. Calvin, *Institutes,* 3.21.1.

15. Barth, *Church Dogmatics,* IV.1, 563.

16. In questioning the rhetoric of choice, I am focusing on the looming prospect of genetic engineering as well as a modern tendency to "disown" children if they make the wrong choices and steer too far from familial expectations. In no way should this understanding of election be taken as a critique of the "pro-choice" movement. The knotty question of abortion is complex and resists the sloganeering of Christian conservatives. It concerns the multiple issues of when life begins, what voice women have in their own sexual and reproductive lives, and the relative inhospitality of contemporary society to women and children. If there is a question of a child's life in the issue of abortion, it must—in my understanding—be considered *nascent* life. And this question of nascent life must be considered within the wider and enormously complex set of social, sexual, and cultural circumstances that the so-called "right to life" movement often ignores. The embryo, in other words, can never be considered in isolation from the multiple lives—most importantly that of the pregnant woman—that surround it. When considered within the larger nexus of human relationships, there will undoubtedly be times when abortion offers some hope under painful circumstances. Rarely, however, will it be an easy decision for the pregnant woman and those close to her. The understanding of election I am advocating focuses on the children who are with us right here, right now, whose voices, strange as it may seem, often drown in the clamor of those who argue on behalf of "life," as if those who disagree with them have no regard for it.

17. For Calvin, moreover, this was not a question divorced from his own life. Calvin did not have a biological child that survived beyond infancy, and adopted—by a pledge of support—the two children from his wife, Idelette de Bure's previous marriage. See Barbara Pitkin, "'The Heritage of the Lord:'" Children in the Theology of John Calvin," in *The Child in Christian Thought,* Marcia J. Bunge, ed. (Grand Rapids: Wm. B. Eerdmans, 2001), 160–61.

18. Calvin, *Institutes,* 3.22.7.

19. Cynthia Rigby offers some helpful reflections on how Christians might conceive the nurture of children as a communal, rather than maternal, calling alone: "The call to self denial . . . might mean that all of us who are not mothers are called beyond our preconceptions about who is responsible for children and to consider what we are called to do to nurture the children we have covenanted to support." "Exploring Our Hesitation: Feminist Theologies and the Nurture of Children," *Theology Today* 56, no. 4 (2000): 551.

20. Lynlea Rodger, "The Infancy Stories of Matthew and Luke: An Examination of the Child as a Theological Metaphor," *Horizons in Biblical Theology* 19, no. 1 (1997): 74.

21. Moltmann, "Child and Childhood as Metaphors of Hope," 600.

22. Augustine suggested that infants manifest sin through tears: "It can hardly be right for a child, even at that age, to cry for everything. . . . I have myself seen jealousy in a baby and know what it means. He was not old enough to talk, but whenever he saw his foster-brother at the breast, he would grow pale with envy," *Confessions,* trans. R. S. Pine-Coffin (New York: Penguin Books, 1961), 27–8.

23. Pamela D. Couture, *Seeing Children, Seeing God: A Practical Theology of Children and Poverty* (Nashville: Abingdon, 2000), 13.

24. John Wesley, "On Zeal," in *John Wesley's Sermons: An Anthology,* Albert C. Outler and Richard P. Heitzenrater, eds. (Nashville: Abingdon, 1991), 468.

25. Jacquelyn Grant, *White Women's Christ and Black Women's Jesus: Feminist Christology and Womanist Response* (Atlanta: Scholars Press, 1989), 213.

26. Couture, *Seeing Children,* 53.

27. Robert Coles, *The Spiritual Life of Children* (Boston: Houghton Mifflin, 1990), 334.

28. Ibid., 329.

29. Bonnie Miller–McLemore writes, "In the best of circumstances, children possess an inexplicable *joie de vivre,* however short its duration, that emerges from living fully in the present." *Also a Mother: Work and Family as Theological Dilemma* (Nashville: Abingdon, 1994), 154.

30. Bonaventure, *The Soul's Journey Into God,* Ewert Cousins, trans. (New York: Paulist Press, 1978), 114–15.

31. Heim, *Depth of the Riches,* 203.

32. During the Holocaust, children played even in the death camps. George Eisen writes: "The contradictions were enormous. The medium that could create a vague and tenuous bridge over the abyss between a hazy past and a stark presence was the games and play activities springing up spontaneously even in the middle of Auschwitz. They helped the children assimilate the horrors on their own terms and accommodate their psychic universe to the environment. It was perhaps not a coincidence that almost no suicide was recorded among children or teenagers, in contrast to that of the adult population. One of the likely reasons for this anomaly was that these children possessed an ability and imagination, which were rarely found among adults, to enact atrocity through play." Eisen, *Children and Play in the Holocaust: Games Among the Shadows* (Amherst, MA: University of Massachusetts Press, 1988), 81.

33. Horace Bushnell, *Christian Nurture* (New York: Charles Scribner's Sons, 1908), 10.

34. Ibid., 39.

35. Ibid., 339.

36. Ibid., 339–41.

37. Ibid., 341.

38. Ibid., 340.

39. Ibid., 340.

40. Rita Nakashima Brock recapitulates this understanding of play by suggesting that "play is not frivolous or trivial, but life-sustaining. It is

the basis of freedom, creativity, and spontaneity." *Journeys By Heart: A Christology of Erotic Power* (New York: Crossroad, 1988), 36.

41. Bushnell's daughter, Mary Bushnell Cheney, claims that "it was while watching the play of his own children with a graceful kitten he conceived the idea which animates his Work and Play; and in the same manner he drew from his own home experience the child-loving chapter on 'Plays and Pastimes,' in his *Christian Nurture*," Bushnell, *The Life and Letters of Horace Bushnell*, ed. Mary Bushnell Cheney (New York: Harper & Brothers, 1880), 453.

42. The documentary film, "Inside Out: Portraits of Children," directed by Joanna Lipper, suggests that the imagination of children is cross-cultural, pervading the play of children in countless corners of the globe.

43. This understanding of Coleridge is inspired most directly by a lecture given by Professor Peter Hodgson at Vanderbilt University, February 13, 1996. See also Samuel Coleridge, *Aids to Reflection,* ed. John Beer (Princeton, NJ: Princeton University Press, 1993), 79.

44. Jesus' parables are likewise exercises in the imagination, inviting us to envision a new world.

45. Miller-McLemore, *Also a Mother,* 156.

46. Simone Weil, *Waiting for God* (New York: Harper & Row, 1973), 105.

47. Robert Coles's study, *The Spiritual Life of Children,* which I have cited in this chapter, also suggests as much. See pages 303–35.

48. Weil, *Waiting for God,* 111–12.

49. Rodger, "The Infancy Stories of Matthew and Luke," 78.

CHAPTER 4

1. UNICEF, *The State of the World's Children 2002* (New York: UNICEF, 2002), 72.

2. Ibid., 63.

3. Ibid., 39.

4. National Center for Children in Poverty, Columbia University, http://cpmcnet.columbia.edu/dept/nccp/ycpf.html.

5. Marian Wright Edelman, quoted in *2001 The State of America's Children* (Washington, DC: Children's Defense Fund, 2001), xiv.

6. Ibid., x.

7. Ibid., 2.

8. *State of the World's Children 2002*, 16.

9. Ibid.

10. Ibid., 40. Moreover, "an estimated 1.4 million children under the age of 15 [live] with HIV worldwide." Ibid.

11. Ibid., 52.

12. Ibid., 61.

13. Ibid., 52.

14. Couture, *Seeing Children*, 42–3.

15. Bushnell, *Christian Nurture*, 406.

16. Adrienne Rich, *Of Woman Born: Motherhood as Experience and Institution* (New York: W.W. Norton, 1995).

17. *State of the World's Children 2002*, 38.

18. *State of America's Children*, 81.

19. Ibid., 80.

20. Ibid., 100.

21. Ibid., xiv.

22. Couture, *Seeing Children*, 34.

23. Figures gathered by Amnesty International. See http://web
.amnesty.org/library/index/engact500042003. The United Nations Declaration on the Rights of the Child contains a provision on the prohibition of such executions. All UN member states have signed the document except the United States and Somalia.

24. Jan Oberg, quoted in Walter Lowe, "Militarism, Evil, and the Reign of God," in *Reconstructing Christian Theology*, Rebecca S. Chopp and Mark Lewis Taylor, eds. (Minneapolis: Fortress Press, 1994), 195.

25. *State of the World's Children*, 42.

26. Lowe, "Militarism, Evil, and the Reign of God," 196.

27. *State of America's Children*, xxviii.

28. One sign of hope is the 1989 United Nations Convention on the Rights of the Child, which presents an ambitious agenda for increased

immunization, the eradication of child labor, and stemming the tide of violence. All UN member states, except Somalia and the United States, have now ratified the convention.

29. Herbert Anderson and Susan B. W. Johnson, *Regarding Children: A New Respect for Childhood and Families* (Louisville: Westminster John Knox, 1994), 2.

30. Ibid, 40.

31. For a compelling articulation of children as sinful, see Miller-McLemore, *Let the Children,* 57–81. The present chapter echoes some of Miller-McLemore's claims, particularly as it considers children as sinned against.

32. Luke T. Johnson, *The Writings of the New Testament: An Interpretation* (Philadelphia: Fortress Press, 1986), 322.

33. E. P. Sanders, *Paul* (New York: Oxford University Press, 1991), 76.

34. Robert R. Williams, "Sin and Evil," in *Christian Theology,* ed. Peter C. Hodgson and Robert H. King (Minneapolis: Fortress Press, 1994), 199.

35. Augustine, "On Nature and Grace," in *The Nicene and Post-Nicene Fathers,* ed. Philip Schaff (Grand Rapids: Wm. B. Eerdmans, 1956), 132.

36. Eugene TeSelle, *Augustine the Theologian* (New York: Herder and Herder, 1970), 144.

37. Augustine, "On Original Sin," in Schaff, *Nicene and Post-Nicene Fathers,* 253.

38. Williams, "Sin and Evil," 203.

39. Augustine, *City of God,* trans. Henry Bettenson (New York: Penguin Books, 1984), 688–89, emphasis mine.

40. John Calvin, *Institutes of the Christian Religion* (1559), 2.1.4.

41. Ibid., 2.1.5.

42. Ibid., 2.3.5.

43. Ibid.

44. Ibid., 2.1.8.

45. See Barbara Pitkin, "The Heritage of the Lord: Children in the Theology of John Calvin," in *The Child in Christian Thought,* ed. Marcia J. Bunge (Grand Rapids: Wm. B. Eerdmans, 2001), 164–69.

46. We will explore this dimension of Calvin in the following chapter.

47. Friedrich Schleiermacher, *The Christian Faith*, ed. H. R. Mackintosh and J. S. Stewart (Edinburgh: T. and T. Clark, 1989), 271.

48. Ibid., 298.

49. Ibid., 301.

50. See Irenaeus, "Against Heresies," in *The Ante-Nicene Fathers*, vol. I, ed. Alexander Roberts and James Donaldson (Grand Rapids: Wm. B. Eerdman's, 1967), 537–42. Paul Tillich is a twentieth-century voice who echoes some Irenaean themes. His interpretation of sin suggests that creation and fall coincide.

51. Rita Nakashima Brock, *Journeys By Heart: A Christology of Erotic Power* (New York: Crossroad, 1988), 7.

52. Ibid.

53. Ibid., 98.

54. For Brock, Christology breaks forth in ecclesiology. The risen Christ is present with the victims of the patriarchy in the life of the community: "The resurrection of Jesus is a powerful image of the need for solidarity among and with victims of oppressive powers. The resurrection affirms that no one person alone can overcome brokenness. . . . The power that gives and sustains life does not flow from a dead and resurrected savior to his followers. Rather, the community sustains life-giving power by its memory of its own brokenheartedness and of those who have suffered and gone before and by its members being courageously and redemptively present to all." Ibid., 103–05.

55. Couture, *Seeing Children*, 62.

56. Miller-McLemore, *Let the Children*, 21.

57. Janet Pais, *Suffer the Children: A Theology of Liberation by a Victim of Child Abuse* (New York: Paulist Press, 1991), 30.

58. Andrew Sung Park and Susan L. Nelson, "Why Do We Need Another Book on the Subject of Sin?" in *The Other Side of Sin: Woundedness from the Perspective of the Sinned-Against,* ed. Andrew Sung Park and Susan L. Nelson (Albany, NY: State University of New York Press, 2001), 13.

59. Ibid., 2.

60. Theodore W. Jennings, Jr., "Reconstructing the Doctrine of Sin," in Park and Nelson, *The Other Side of Sin,* 112.

61. Miller-McLemore, *Let the Children,* 80.

62. Susan L. Nelson, "For Shame, for Shame, the Shame of it All: Postures of Refusal and the Broken Heart," in Park and Nelson, *The Other Side of Sin,* 73.

63. For a graphic narrative of child abuse and the shame that it engenders, see Dorothy Allison, *Bastard Out of Carolina* (New York: Plume, 1993), which documents one girl's experience of sexual abuse, her struggle with depression, and subsequent embrace of her self-worth.

64. Nelson, "For Shame," 77.

65. Ibid., 83–4.

66. Martin Luther King Jr., "Letter from Birmingham Jail—April 16, 1963," in *Afro-American Religious History: A Documentary Witness,* ed. Milton C. Sernett (Durham, NC: Duke University Press, 1985), 431.

67. Douglas Sturm, "On the Suffering and Rights of Children: Toward a Theology of Childhood Liberation," *Cross Currents* 42, no. 2 (Summer 1992), 170.

68. Paul's nascent ecclesiology, as demonstrated in many of his letters, displays keen attention to the interrelation of all members of the church. Whenever one member asserts superiority, the whole body is diminished. Whenever one suffers, the whole suffers. "If one member suffers, all suffer together with it; if one member is honored, all rejoice together with it" (1 Cor. 12:26).

69. Nelson, "For Shame," 84.

70. Susan L. Nelson, *Healing the Broken Heart: Sin, Alienation and the Gift of Grace* (St. Louis: Chalice Press, 1998), 80.

71. Andrew Sung Park's work, *The Wounded Heart of God: The Asian Concept of Han and the Christian Doctrine of Sin* (Nashville: Abingdon Press, 1993), is helpful in this regard. Park exposes some of the inadequacies of the classic doctrine of sin, which tends to focus on the moral agent, and suggests that theologians draw on the Asian concept of *han,* the "abysmal experience of pain," which expresses itself in active and passive forms. Ibid., 15.

72. Jennings, "Reconstructing the Doctrine of Sin," 121.

73. John Wesley, "Original Sin," in *John Wesley's Sermons: An Anthology*, ed. Albert C. Outler and Richard P. Heitzenrater (Nashville: Abingdon Press, 1991), 333.

CHAPTER 5

1. The practice of believer's baptism, likewise, can undergird the church's care for infants and children. On this note, Calvin seems to have missed the point, when he suggested that believer's baptism ignored the nurture of children. See Calvin, *Institutes* (1559), 4.16.21–22. For an account of the nurture of children in Anabaptist thought, see Menno Simons, "The Nurture of Children," *The Complete Writings of Menno Simons*, trans. Leonard Verduin (Scottdale, PA: Herald Press, 1956), 947–52. See also Keith Graber Miller, "Complex Innocence, Obligatory Nurturance, and Parental Vigilance: 'The Child' in the Work of Menno Simons," in Bunge, *The Child in Christian Thought*, 194–226.

2. Calvin, *Institutes*, 4.14.1.

3. Ibid., 4.14.6.

4. Ibid., 4.15.1.

5. Ibid., 4.15.20.

6. In ibid., 4.16.31, Calvin describes baptism as "the symbol of their adoption."

7. Calvin uses the image of "family" and "household" to portray the church, most notably in the concluding lines of his defense of infant baptism. See ibid., 4.16.32.

8. Ibid., 4.15.22. The Heidelberg Catechism echoes this strain when it affirms that infants are to be baptized "because they, as well as their parents, are included in the covenant and belong to the people of God." *The Constitution of the Presbyterian Church (U.S.A.), Part I: The Book of Confessions* (Louisville: Office of the General Assembly Presbyterian Church (U.S.A.)), 4.074.

9. Calvin, *Institutes*, 4.16.5.

10. Ibid., 4.16.9.

11. Ibid., 4.16. 32.

12. Milton Mayeroff, *On Caring* (New York: Harper & Row, 1971), 1.

13. Barbara Pitkin, "'The Heritage of the Lord:' Children in the Theology of John Calvin," in Bunge, *The Child in Christian Thought*, 193.

14. In the ancient church, many were baptized nude, a vivid reminder of the believer's rebirth and nakedness before God.

15. For a concise treatment of this "third way" of nonviolence, see Walter Wink, *Jesus and Nonviolence: A Third Way* (Minneapolis: Fortress Press, 2003), 9-36.

16. Another prominent liturgical practice is the sign—or in some communities, kiss—of peace.

17. Stanley Hauerwas, *The Peaceable Kingdom: A Primer in Christian Ethics* (Notre Dame, IN: University of Notre Dame Press, 1983), 108.

18. J. Denny Weaver, *Becoming Anabaptist: The Origin and Significance of Sixteenth-Century Anabaptism* (Scottdale, PA: Herald Press, 1987), 136.

19. Dietrich Philips, "The Church of God," in *Spiritual and Anabaptist Writers*, George H. Williams and Angel M. Mergal, eds. (Philadelphia: Westminster, 1957), 252. In the context of the United States' ongoing "war on terror," peacemakers are often seen as threats to national security. Criticism of the war on Iraq constitutes unpatriotic speech, according to Oval Office spin-doctors. Military spokespersons, encountered daily on news programs, brook little dissent as carnage mounts on all sides.

20. J. Denny Weaver, *Anabaptist Theology in Face of Postmodernity: A Proposal for the Third Millennium* (Telford, PA: Pandora Press, 2000), 35.

21. The concluding chapter of Herbert Anderson and Susan B. W. Johnson's volume, *Regarding Children*, offers a sustained reflection on the church as "sanctuary for childhood." In parts of what follow, I draw from their helpful presentation of a sorely needed image of church.

22. Anderson and Johnson, *Regarding Children*, 112.

23. Eileen W. Lindner, "Toward a Sanctuary Movement," *Church and Society* 91, no. 1 (September/October 2000), 89.

24. The work of Jerome W. Berryman and Sonja M. Stewart represents a welcome contribution in exploring worship with children.

Following the liturgical year, this program allows young children (ages three to six) to explore the prayers, sacraments, and lectionary texts through artwork, storytelling, and their own questions. Each session follows the rhythm of the Sunday service and the cycle of the church year. See Berryman and Stewart, *Young Children and Worship* (Louisville: Westminster John Knox, 1990).

25. Stephen Cherry, "Sanctuary: A Reflection on a Critical Praxis," *Theology* 93 (March–April 1990), 147.

26. Anderson and Johnson, *Regarding Children*, 131.

27. *Constitution of the Presbyterian Church,* 4.120.

28. Ibid., 7.098.

29. Friedrich Schleiermacher, "The Power of Prayer in Relation to Outward Circumstances," in *Friedrich Schleiermacher: Pioneer of Modern Theology*, Keith Clements, ed. (Minneapolis: Fortress Press, 1991), 192.

30. *Constitution of the Presbyterian Church,* 7.293.

31. Coles, *The Spiritual Life of Children*, 334.

CHAPTER 6

1. Karl Rahner, "Ideas for a Theology of Childhood," in *Theological Investigations*, vol. 8 (New York: Herder & Herder, 1971), 34.

2. It is obvious, however, that the age of consumption reaches ever-younger populations. Countless products are marketed with preschoolers in mind, who provide a willing and malleable audience to the messages of television advertising. The products marketed toward children are not only the innocuous baubles of toys and breakfast foods, but include cigarettes and firearms as well.

3. Exposure is the practice of abandoning infants in a public space, with the expectation that a stranger would pick up the child and care for it. Often, exposed infants were raised as slaves or prostitutes. See Judith M. Gundry-Volf, "The Least and the Greatest: Children in the New Testament," in Bunge, *The Child in Christian Thought*, 31–4. In his provocative work, *The History of Childhood* (New York: Psychohistory Press, 1974), Lloyd deMause argues, "The further back in history one goes, the lower the level of child care, and the more likely children are

to be killed, abandoned, beaten, terrorized, and sexually abused." He cites a letter of a Greek Hilarion to his wife Alis (1 B.C.E.) as typical of the age's frankness on infant exposure: "If, as may well happen, you give birth to a child, if it is a boy let it live, if it is a girl, expose it." For deMause, this "infanticidal mode" of parent-child relations extended from antiquity to the fourth century, C.E. (Ibid., 1, 26, 51).

4. Gundry-Volf, "The Least and the Greatest," 39.

5. Ibid., 40.

6. Rahner, "Ideas for a Theology of Childhood," 37–8. I have altered the translator's rendering of Rahner's terms, opting for more gender-inclusive language.

7. Ibid., 40.

8. Ibid., 42. Note here how Rahner emphasizes play as integral to childhood, a theme that echoes chapter 3.

9. Ibid., 35–6.

10. Laura Ingalls Wilder captures this endurance of the present, which is characteristic of many children's understandings of time: "When the fiddle had stopped singing Laura called out softly, 'What are days of auld lang syne, Pa?'

'They are the days of a long time ago, Laura,' Pa said. 'Go to sleep, now.'

But Laura lay awake a little while, listening to Pa's fiddle softly playing in the Big Woods. She looked at Pa sitting on the bench by the hearth, the fire-light gleaming on his brown hair and beard and glistening on the honey-brown fiddle. She looked at Ma, gently rocking and knitting.

She thought to herself, 'This is now.'

She was glad that the cosy house, and Pa and Ma and the fire-light and the music, were now. They could not be forgotten, she thought, because now is now. It can never be a long time ago." Wilder, *Little House in the Big Woods* (New York: HarperCollins, 1953), 237–8.

11. Rahner, "Theology of Childhood," 36.

12. Mary Ann Hinsdale echoes this theme in her interpretation of Rahner: "For adults to attain the openness of children (which is what

the kingdom of heaven requires), conversion is necessary. Yet, this conversion is only to become what we already are—children. Paradoxically, none of us know what childhood means at the beginning of our lives. It is only at the end of a lifetime of God-given repentance and conversion that we will be able to realize that childhood in which we receive the kingdom of God and thus become God's children." "'Infinite Openness to the Infinite': Karl Rahner's Contribution to Modern Catholic Thought on the Child," in Bunge, *The Child in Christian Thought*, 426.

13. Gundry-Volf, "The Least and the Greatest," 45.

14. Ibid., 60. For a similar account of Jesus' blessing of children and the care of children as ecclesial practice, see Miller-McLemore, *Let the Children*, 94–104; 161–170.

Related Titles from The Pilgrim Press

ALSO BY DAVID H. JENSEN

IN THE COMPANY OF OTHERS
A Dialogical Christology

"David H. Jensen ... offers a portrait of Christ that, while retaining its distinctiveness and centrality for Christians, welcomes others in the heartiest fashion possible: the self-emptying Christ is an open invitation to others. . . . It is difficult to imagine a more fruitful basis for interreligious dialogue."
—from the Foreword by Sallie McFague

"Jensen has transformed Christology from a roadblock to a launching pad for interreligious dialogue. . . . Jensen's study will surely bring both tough new questions and exciting new directions to the contemporary discussion of a Christian theology of religions."
—Paul K. Knitter, author of *No Other Name?, One Earth Many Religions,* and *Introducing Theologies of Religion.*

ISBN 0-8298-1420-5/Paper/224 pages/$16.00

CHILDREN TOGETHER
Teaching Girls and Boys to Value Themselves and Each Other

KATHRYN GOERING REID AND KEN HAWLEY

Children Together will help the church teach children about inequality and discrimination and help children learn to value themselves and others for who they are. Each age-appropriate lesson covers topics such as learning to work together, exploring individual potential, media and stereotypes, and sexual harassment.

ISBN 0-8298-1380-2/Paper/114 pages/$15.00

MAKING A HOME FOR FAITH
Nurturing the Spiritual Life of Your Children

ELIZABETH F. CALDWELL

Talking about faith with children can be challenging. In this book, Elizabeth Caldwell offers guidance to parents and caregivers who want to take an active role in the faith development of their children. By modeling their own faith, Caldwell believes they can encourage their children's faith. Designed for use by individuals and groups, the book includes reflection questions in each chapter to foster dialogue in variety of settings. Church leaders who work with children will find this a valuable resource as well.

ISBN 0-8298-1370-5/Paper/118 pages/$15.00

LEAVING HOME WITH FAITH
Nurturing the Spiritual Life of Our Youth

ELIZABETH F. CALDWELL

A companion and continuation to *Making A Home For Faith,* Caldwell discusses ways in which youth can continue to grow in faith after leaving home.

ISBN 0-8298-1504-X/Paper/128 pages/$15.00

PRACTICING DISCERNMENT WITH YOUTH
A Transformative Youth Ministry Approach

DAVID F. WHITE

In the last half-century, the expectations, imaginations, and practices of youth ministry are more likely to develop away from the unique and particular setting of a congregation. David White develops the notion of practicing discernment among youth as a means of returning the responsibility for youth ministry to local congregations and youth groups. The author provides a new understanding of youth ministry as a way of responding to the particular wounds, blessings, gifts, and charisms of youth and congregations.

Practicing Discernment with Youth is a part of the new series, *Youth Ministry Alternatives*

ISBN 0-8298-1631-3/Paper/224 pages/$24.00

WHOSE KIDS ARE THEY ANYWAY?
Religion and Morality in America's Public Schools

RAYMOND R. ROBERTS

In the debate over moral education in public schools, Raymond Roberts' argument is shaped by five different understandings of religion. The author recommends a sixth mediating position where all children belong to a plurality of spheres—to parents, to the public, and to God. Each sphere is required to play a critical role in the nurture and education of children.

ISBN 0-8298-1457-4/Cloth/208 pages/$19.00

DAUGHTERS ARISE
A Christian Retreat Resource for Girls Approaching Womanhood

GLORIA KOLL, DONNA HUMPHREYS AND SALLY WINDECKER

Daughters Arise is a guidebook for creating uplifting retreats for girls of all cultures entering womanhood as well as their mothers or mentors. It uses drama, music, art, movement, ceremony, and story to nourish each participant's spirit. The activities celebrate what it means to be a daughter of God.

ISBN 0-8298-1469-8/Paper/Workbook/256 pages/$25.00

To order these or any other books from The Pilgrim Press, call or write to:

THE PILGRIM PRESS
700 PROSPECT AVENUE
CLEVELAND, OH 44115-1100

Phone orders: 800·537·3394 (M–F, 8:30 AM–4:30 PM ET)
Fax orders: 216·736·2206

Please include shipping charges of $5.00 for the first book and 75¢ for each additional book. Or order from our web site at www.thepilgrimpress.com.

Prices subject to change without notice.